1997

NEW DIRECTIONS FOR INSTITUTIO

N

Patrick T. Terenzini
The Pennsylvania State University
EDITOR-IN-CHIEF

Ellen Earle Chaffee
North Dakota University System
ASSOCIATE EDITOR

Containing Costs and Improving Productivity in Higher Education

Carol S. Hollins
John Tyler Community College

EDITOR

Number 75, Fall 1992

JOSSEY-BASS PUBLISHERS
San Francisco

CONTAINING COSTS AND IMPROVING PRODUCTIVITY IN HIGHER EDUCATION
Carol S. Hollins (ed.)
New Directions for Institutional Research, no. 75
Volume XVIV, Number 3
Patrick T. Terenzini, Editor-in-Chief
Ellen Earle Chaffee, Associate Editor

Microfilm copies of issues and articles are available in 16mm and 35mm, as well as microfiche in 105mm, through University Microfilms Inc., 300 North Zeeb Road, Ann Arbor, Michigan 48106.

LC 87-645339   ISSN 0217-0579   ISBN 1-55542-736-7

NEW DIRECTIONS FOR INSTITUTIONAL RESEARCH is part of The Jossey-Bass Adult and Higher Education Series and is published quarterly by Jossey-Bass Inc., Publishers, 350 Sansome Street, San Francisco, California 94104-1310 (publication number USPS 098-830). Second-class postage paid at San Francisco, California, and at additional mailing offices. POSTMASTER: Send address changes to New Directions for Institutional Research, Jossey-Bass Inc., Publishers, 350 Sansome Street, San Francisco, California 94104-1310.

SUBSCRIPTIONS for 1992 cost $45.00 for individuals and $60.00 for institutions, agencies, and libraries.

EDITORIAL CORRESPONDENCE should be sent to the Editor-in-Chief, Patrick T. Terenzini, Center for the Study of Higher Education, The Pennsylvania State University, 403 South Allen Street, Suite 104, University Park, Pennsylvania 16801-5202.

Photograph of the library by Michael Graves at San Juan Capistrano by Chad Slattery © 1984. All rights reserved.

The paper used in this journal is acid-free and meets the strictest guidelines in the United States for recycled paper (50 percent recycled waste, including 10 percent post-consumer waste). Manufactured in the United States of America.

THE ASSOCIATION FOR INSTITUTIONAL RESEARCH was created in 1966 to benefit, assist, and advance research leading to improved understanding, planning, and operation of institutions of higher education. Publication policy is set by its Publications Board.

For information about the Association for Institutional Research, write to the following address:

AIR Executive Office
314 Stone Building
Florida State University
Tallahassee, FL 32306-3038

(904) 644-4470

CONTENTS

EDITOR'S NOTES

Escalating college costs, decreased productivity, and a perceived decline in the quality of undergraduate instruction represent grave concerns for federal and state officials, governing and coordinating boards, the media, and the public community. Not only are external audiences questioning institutional viability but persons within the academy are inquiring about rising costs and acknowledging difficulty in assessing institutional impact. Critics charge that although college costs have skyrocketed, students are being shortchanged by faculty who savor research and publication more than quality teaching.

The inverse relationship between college costs and productivity is a topic that has dominated the higher education agenda in recent years; in fact, it has been called "the issue of the decade." With many institutions facing unprecedented cutbacks, *Money* magazine has referred to this as "the decade of reckoning" for America's colleges and universities (Kobliner, 1992, p. 7). One authority remarked that "public colleges are at a crossroads," citing their low priority for state funds (Davies, 1991).

Why do attempts to analyze costs and increase productivity remain so elusive? How are institutions repositioning themselves to address their fiscal challenges? Are the strategies being employed primarily short-term in hope of more promising economic times, or are institutions demonstrating a genuine commitment to examining priorities in order to achieve long-term improvements? What distinctions are there in retrenchment and repositioning activities underway at public research universities versus private or smaller public colleges? How might institutional researchers, planners, and budget analysts assist their institutions in curtailing costs and reallocating resources?

This volume, *Containing Costs and Improving Productivity in Higher Education*, examines these questions along with an array of factors that affect higher education costs and efficiencies. A number of illustrations are provided for consideration by decision makers charged with allocating costs and improving productivity in higher education.

The conceptual framework used in this volume was developed by William F. Massy and Robert Zemsky (1990) to examine the dynamics of increasing costs and declining productivity in higher education. They advised that the most appropriate response to higher education's condition is to downsize the "administrative lattice," to redirect the "academic ratchet" of specialization, and to "grow by substitution." The administrative lattice refers to the proliferation and retrenchment of staff at colleges and universities. The connotation here is not just numerical increases but also their influence on an institution's operations and costs.

1

The academic ratchet points to a marked shift by faculty from the overarching goals of an institution toward those of an academic specialty, which leads to an increased emphasis on research and publication and a deemphasis of teaching. Growth by substitution assumes that resources are limited, and that promoting growth in one area requires a corresponding reduction in another.

In Chapter One, John A. Dunn, Jr., provides the results of a recent survey on cost containment that seem to indicate that institutions are not viewing the current fiscal crisis as a long-term problem. He concludes that although there are no internal incentives to control costs, costs can and will be constrained by external factors.

Paul T. Brinkman, in Chapter Two, outlines a complex set of factors that influences higher education costs. His typology suggests that effective cost containment strategies, of the magnitude desired, cannot take place solely at the local institutional level. Nonetheless, institutions must play a significant role in higher-level discussions about college costs and suggest ways to achieve greater efficiencies.

Inputs, products, and quality are hard to define and measure in higher education. Notwithstanding, in Chapter Three, Jeffrey L. Gilmore and Duc-Le To examine the relationship between inputs and outputs through several studies of institutional productivity.

In Chapter Four, Mary Jo Maydew proposes that cost containment strategies originate with administrative programs and services that support instruction. She suggests that an administrative retrenchment plan be preceded by a strong and cooperative management team, a common understanding of an institution's priorities, and the adoption of an institutional rather than a territorial perspective.

Michael F. Middaugh and David E. Hollowell conduct a case study that demonstrates the effect of the academic ratchet and administrative lattice in Chapter Five. In addition, they present a framework for conducting productivity analyses and implementing cost containment strategies.

Granted that the University of Michigan (UM) benefits immensely from its institutional autonomy, other college and university officials can learn from UM's efforts to contain and reallocate costs and to enhance quality and revenues. Marilyn G. Knepp, in Chapter Six, provides a case study that summarizes improvement initiatives undertaken by UM during the 1980s.

Although no one is suggesting that reallocation is an easy task, Richard B. Hoffman, in Chapter Seven, shares the approach taken by one independent, liberal arts institution. He urges the avoidance of hasty, stopgap measures, which have characterized the responses of so many institutions. He advocates a long-term investment in institutional research and planning in order to provide advance warning of impending crises.

An ultimate aim of college and university decision makers is to achieve improvements in both quality and productivity, which is the objective of Total Quality Management (TQM) programs. In Chapter Eight, Mary Ann Heverly and Robert A. Cornesky examine the effects of long-term use of TQM to increase productivity and decrease costs.

Finally, in Chapter Nine, I summarize the suggestions of the authors of the preceding chapters. Emphasis is placed on implementation of strategies that will have a long-term impact on institutional operations.

The summons to "do more with less" is one that few of us will readily answer. Nonetheless, in view of higher education's fiscal crises, we must explore every possible avenue in order to continue to meet the changing needs of our constituents. We simply must do so with fewer resources.

Carol S. Hollins
Editor

References

Davies, G. K. "Public Colleges at a Crossroads." *Roanoke Times and World News,* Oct. 11, 1991, p. A11.

Kobliner, B. "The Budget Crunch Hits the Campuses." In *1992 Money College Guide.* New York: Time Magazine Company, 1992.

Massy, W. F., and Zemsky, R. *The Dynamics of Academic Productivity.* (J. R. Mingle, comp.) Denver, Colo.: State Higher Education Executive Officers, 1990.

CAROL S. HOLLINS is coordinator of institutional research at John Tyler Community College, Chester, Virginia.

Colleges and universities have no built-in incentives to control costs, but external constraints outside academe will continue to force difficult decisions.

Retrench or Else: Public and Private Institutional Responses

John A. Dunn, Jr.

The Urgent Versus the Important

First, a minor example. In helping plan a capital campaign at Tufts University a number of years ago, I asked each of the school deans to rank-order their fund-raising needs. Sensitive to Tufts' rapidly rising tuition rates, the deans all put student financial aid at the top. Yet, over the course of the campaign, they requested program enhancement funds (lab renovations, specialized equipment, new program support, incremental faculty, and so on) far more often than they did funds to constrain costs or to aid students. I am not criticizing the deans; they were trying their best to respond to legitimate and pressing needs. In the long run, however, we may have let the urgent crowd out the important.

Now take a larger example: the costs of higher education. Why is it that higher education expenditures and tuitions rose so fast in the last decade? Howard Bowen (1980, pp. 19–20) succinctly described the force that drove the change: "The dominant goals of institutions are educational excellence, prestige, and influence. . . . In quest of [these goals] there is virtually no limit to the amount of money an institution could spend for seemingly fruitful educational ends. . . . Each institution raises all the money it can. . . . Each institution spends all the money it raises." Simply put, the internal pressures in an institution are for expansion of spending; it will continually expand its spending, subject only to availability of funds and to internal constraints related to its mission and imposed by institutional leadership, or to external constraints imposed by market conditions. In effect, there is no internal motivation for cost containment. The institution that holds back on tuition increases or requests for state support when it does not have to simply has less revenue to pay for desirable programs than does its competitor down the street.

During the feel-good 1980s, there seemed to be little reason not to increase spending. Despite predictions of demographic declines, more and more students enrolled. The economy was on a self-indulgent spending spree; parents seemed to think it would go on forever and were willing to pay whatever it took to enroll their children in the best schools. Most states outside the oil-dependent South were reasonably prosperous and growing. In our institutions we found all sorts of pressing needs: rebuilding salary levels for faculty, upgrading neglected plant and equipment, keeping up with the explosive growth of the disciplines and of technology, adding staff to provide more and better support and administrative services, and adding facilities so as to compete better with schools in the same league. All of these were urgent; some of them may even have been important.

We paid for all of these expenditures in the private sector by sharply increasing tuition charges, and in the public sector by rapidly expanding appropriations. Some schools such as Boston University, Kalamazoo College, and Tulane University took advantage of the opportunity to reposition themselves, moving their tuitions to a whole new competitive league. A few leadership schools like Stanford and Northwestern exercised considerable restraint; other, less prestigious schools were competitively constrained. In the public arena, many state colleges fought to upgrade their status to universities, and many universities fought for the resources to become doctorate-granting and research institutions.

In the midst of this urgency, we did not choose to see the important things that were happening around us. The booming economy, built largely on unsustainable rates of expenditure, was headed for a bust. The rich in our society were getting richer, but incomes in the middle class were barely holding even, and the numbers of the poor were growing rapidly. Our college and university expenditures and charges were increasing far faster than the incomes of the families that we were supposed to be serving, and social attitudes toward higher education began to shift. The federal government was backing out of its commitment to student aid. We thought William Bennett (then secretary of the Department of Education) and other critics caused the social changes; in retrospect, they were just harbingers. As we were enthusiastically indulging our urgencies, the important social ground on which we exist had shifted under our feet.

Perception Versus Reality in Cost Escalation

To see what was happening during the 1980s, it is useful to place the decade in a longer time period. Although it is dangerous to argue a

Figure 1.1. National Median Family Income and Cost of
Attending Tufts University in Constant 1990 Dollars
(Deflated by the Consumer Price Index)

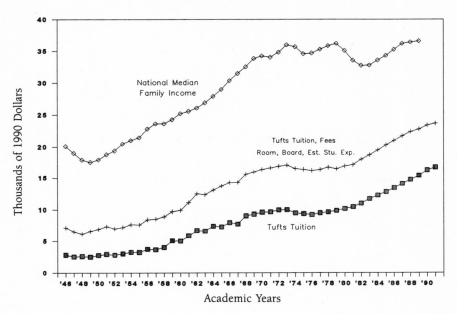

general theory from one institution's data, a case study can dramatize the trends.

Let's look at what has happened to the cost of attending Tufts University since World War II (see Figure 1.1). Tuition and the full cost of attendance rose in real terms with remarkable consistency. They were held down somewhat in the 1970s by skimping on faculty salaries and physical plant upkeep. And they rose more steeply in the 1980s, catching up on salaries and plant maintenance and compensating for cutbacks in federal student aid.

Two factors drove this increase. First, as has often been observed, colleges and universities have to pay competitive wages to keep good people, but they lack industry's ability to offset those increases with gains in productivity. This factor drives costs up 1 to 2 percent above inflation each year. Second, colleges and universities are idea factories. Disciplines evolve, requiring added staff; scientific and technological advances require ever more expensive equipment; libraries need to find access to more materials. This factor probably adds another 1 to 2 percent per year to college costs.

The other major message in Figure 1.1 is that national median family income stopped growing in the early 1970s. College costs rose in real terms for several decades after World War II. Since real incomes climbed as well, the cost of a good private college education held constant as a percentage of income. Since the latter part of the 1970s, however, the fraction of income needed to cover college cost has risen sharply, in part because college costs have risen, but in large measure because incomes failed to grow.

While we must be critical of our own tendencies in higher education to indulge the urgent and self-gratifying at the risk of the important, we should recognize that the same tendencies characterized the whole society during the 1980s.

The Bowen Thesis: Measuring Inputs, Not Outputs

Bowen (1980) describes our goals as "educational excellence, prestige, and influence." On first reading, the list is reasonable. Much of what we try to do, at least in pursuit of the first of these goals, is clearly desirable.

From the cost constraint point of view, the problem is that we have no agreement on the output measures by which to judge our progress toward those goals. Despite the hoary jokes, it is not clear that it takes two Princeton graduates to do the work of a Yale graduate or half of a Harvard graduate. Therefore, we measure inputs, resources used. We look at the number of faculty members per student; the publication record and distinguished research accomplishments of the faculty; the physical environment, in trees and green space and equipment and specialized facilities; the size and range of the library collection; the size of the budget and of the endowment; even the records of the athletic teams. We measure prestige, influence, and educational excellence, in other words, in terms of the amount of resources devoted to them. If our own self-image depends on how much we get to spend, no wonder we push to spend more!

In this context it is easy to understand why state legislators and others have pushed so hard for accountability, assessment, graduation rates, faculty credit-hour productivity, and statewide and even national testing. They understand the nature of the vicious circle of prestige and spending and want to find output measures to substitute for higher education's input measures.

In Whose Interest Is It to Constrain Costs?

An implication of Bowen's thesis is that no constituencies in higher education (at least not within institutions) have a built-in interest in cost constraint.

Prospective Students. For some students, the choice of college is dictated by the fact that the local institution is the only feasible alternative. For many, however, it is a complex decision. In part, it is a rational process of matching the student's skills, interests and ability to pay with the school's offerings and charges. There are subtler factors as well. Each institution carries a relatively commonly perceived set of connotations in terms of intellectual rigor, social prestige, athletic prowess, religious or sectarian flavor, conservative or liberal spirit, and the like. The decision is emotional, involving the student's aspirations and self-image, and is often driven by whether the student believes that he or she can feel comfortable on the campus.

In terms of price, there is a common perception, as applicable to the public as to the private sector, that one gets what one pays for. Institutions understand this perfectly well and build sophisticated marketing campaigns on this basis. Several schools have aggressively moved their tuition levels upward, gaining both additional resources for programmatic use and enhanced reputations in the marketplace.

Current Students. Current students do, of course, protest increases in student charges, often with vigor. But they often protest even more vociferously any cuts in programs, even though those cuts might avert tuition increases.

Faculty. Faculty members conscientiously want to do the best possible job, and they also want to get ahead in their profession. With respect to educational programs, this drive for excellence translates into additional faculty positions so as to cover the various fields better, lower course loads so as to prepare the classes better and do more research in their fields, more teaching assistants for close instruction, smaller classes to permit more discussion, better equipment, and so on. The drive for advancement translates into requests for released time and financial support for research and publication, into professionalization that moves away from such miscellaneous duties as advising, and into more active involvement in professional conferences and associations.

Administrators and Key Staff. While some senior administrators may be closer to the institution's financial numbers than are the faculty, they have their own imperatives. To carry out their own responsibilities more effectively, they need better academic and administrative computer support, more sophisticated human resources personnel and programs (and legal staffs) to respond to ever more complex regulations and benefits programs, facility audits and skilled consulting to determine how best to use and maintain the plant assets, better cost information to manage tighter budgets, and more development officers and alumni relations and public relations people to improve the institution's image and flow of support (Middaugh and Hollowell, 1991, p. 10).

Board of Directors. The board's role is to ensure that the institution carries out its mission and that it is well enough managed to allow it to continue to do so in perpetuity. This means that the conscientious board member must be a critic if the school fails to live up to its mission, and an advocate for continued sound management. Some colleges and universities have an especially strong service mission stemming from a religious or social purpose that underscores the importance of keeping charges down.

Donors. Donors want to be proud of the institution. They like to see it grow in prestige, educational excellence, and reputation. If they are alumni, the value of their own degree rises proportionately with the reputation of the school. Like prospective students, donors gain in self-image by their association with schools that are "the best."

Governor and Legislators. Colleges and universities occasionally make useful whipping boys for political candidates to excoriate, but by and large public officials want to be proud of their institutions. They understand the role of higher education in the civic and social awareness, the cultural richness, and, most important, the economic well-being of their area. They understand that it takes resources to become the best, although they occasionally suspect waste and fraud. And, subject to competing budget constraints, they generally try to see that requested additional resources are made available.

What Constraints Are There?

If institutions seek educational excellence, prestige, and influence through ever-increasing expenditures, and if there are no constituencies with a built-in interest in constraining cost, what forces limit institutional spending?

Unavailability of Money to Spend. In the public sector, legislatures and state higher education boards have very effective control over spending, since they provide the great majority of the funds to the institutions under their purview. Moreover, those institutions are typically prohibited from running deficits and usually are required to return unused funds. Only a few public institutions such as the University of Michigan or the University of California at Berkeley have endowments or other external resources that make significant contributions to their budgets and thus increase their flexibility. State constraints on resources generally result from economic difficulties but reflect social concerns as well. When state tax revenues fall, all public services may suffer. Increasingly, however, public disenchantment with higher education and perceived priorities for other services such as health care, crime prevention, and primary and secondary education have made for disproportionate cuts in the funding of public colleges and universities.

For private institutions, constraints on revenues come from competitive limits in the number of students that they can attract, the tuition they can charge (net of financial aid), and the funds they receive from donors past (endowment) or present. As with public institutions, both economic and social factors are involved. Demographic changes may shrink the pool of potential students, competition among similar private institutions or between public and private ones may require massive tuition discounting, and donors may cut back on their giving if they disagree with something the institution is doing, if they perceive it to be wasteful, or if they are, by their own economic circumstances, unable to contribute as much.

Self-Discipline. Up to this point, the analysis has been flavored by heavy doses of economic determinism and institutional self-interest. My description of the behavior of higher education institutions is a general one. It clearly does not capture the reality for all of the more than three thousand U.S. colleges and universities, public and private, with very different missions and in different areas of the country. Even within the relatively narrow segment of private high-tuition schools, a study of tuition trends over the last five years (Dunn, 1991c) showed conflicting patterns: In general, research and doctoral universities increased their student charges more slowly than did comprehensive universities. In general, lower-priced institutions increased their charges faster than did top-priced schools, although the absolute gap between them did not narrow. But the programmatic needs, the competitive situation, and the aspirations of the particular schools were more important determinants of changes in student charges than were mission (determined by the Carnegie Commission classification) or current tuition level.

Some institutions have shown considerable self-discipline over the years, not spending all the revenue that was available to them. For several decades, Harvard University showed on its operating statement a line for "endowment income availed of"; the balance was plowed back into capital. Boston College and other schools have systematically built their endowments and funded new construction by holding operating expenses below revenues and using the surpluses for these purposes. In fact, several studies have suggested that transfers of funds into endowments account for a larger share of the variance in endowment growth between institutions than does investment performance or drawdown rate (Dunn, 1991a; Frances and Williamson, 1992).

While some institutions keep their tuition rates low because of either state requirements or special mission (for example, theological schools), or have to do so for competitive reasons, others have chosen to increase tuitions more slowly than they might have. Stanford and Northwestern are among these.

Finally, some universities should be given credit for foresighted planning. The University of Michigan began cost cutting several years ago. The University of Minnesota has adopted a "commitment to focus," and the University of Wisconsin is downsizing as well. Among private universities, Columbia University and Washington University (Saint Louis) have each cut programs. Georgetown eliminated one of its professional schools.

Predicted Behavior in a Cost Crunch

If Bowen's thesis is on target, how would one expect colleges and universities to act when confronted by a fiscal crunch? First, they deny the reality to avoid loss of self-esteem and external prestige. They ignore danger signs. Enrollment shortfalls catch them by surprise. They do not plan for reductions in tuition rates or in state support, inevitable though those changes may be.

Second, if the problem cannot be denied, they try to solve it by revenue solutions rather than expense cuts. They lobby vigorously for increased appropriations and gifts and seek nontraditional support such as technology parks.

Third, they seek to mask or put off the problem. They engage in creative accounting, shifting costs to off-operating-statement or off-balance-sheet accounts. They begin to use up capital assets by inadequate maintenance of plant, by increasing payout rates from endowment, or even by selling off campus land or buildings.

Fourth, they attempt to cut back as painlessly as possible. There is a recognizable sequence: (1) Cut out-of-pocket expenses: memberships, travel expenses, subscriptions, and so on. (2) If personnel reductions are inevitable, cuts will come first in the administrative areas, protecting the faculty. (3) Cuts will be made across the board where possible; the singling out of specific departments makes enemies and requires public justification of the choices. (4) In the administrative areas, cuts will come where the least flak will result: the newly hired rather than long-term employees, staff positions rather than line, less visible people at the bottom of the hierarchy rather than old friends among the senior administrators.

Fifth, programs will be cut. These programs will be small ones that are not central to the school's mission and that do not have outspoken supporters on the faculty or among donors or legislators. Often the faculty are transferred to other programs; the institution claims program reduction without actually having cut costs!

Finally, faculty personnel may have to be cut, if absolutely inevitable. Again, the least painful approach is desired: eliminate vacant positions and suspend searches before laying off real people, transfer "excess" faculty members to other programs rather than let them go, decline to renew contracts rather than terminate existing contracts, cut non–tenure eligible faculty first, cut nontenured tenure-track faculty next, but only when their contracts are up for renewal; as a last resort, and only if the institution will otherwise go under, cut tenured faculty.

What Has Actually Been Happening by Way of Cost Containment?

In October 1991, the Center for Planning Information (Dunn, 1991b) conducted a mail survey on cost containment, focusing on changes between fiscal year (FY) 1991 and 1992. The questionnaire went to the members of several consortia: the Higher Education Data Sharing Consortium, with 124 private colleges and universities; the Public Universities Information Exchange, with 24 public universities; the Southern University Group, with 32 public universities; and the College and University Library Association, with 8 academic libraries. The response rates by institutional type are presented in Table 1.1. This survey continued a questionnaire administered in April 1991 to essentially the same set of institutions. Neither survey attempted to cover all of higher education or even to constitute a stratified random sample; the results, therefore, may not be generalizable.

Overall, a majority of the institutions surveyed confirmed enrollment increases; however, half of those experiencing decreases in enrollment had not predicted the declines. Like enrollment decreases, budget shortfalls were generally unanticipated. Declining state support was widespread, and tuition rose at most public institutions. Cost containment measures included freezing nonpersonnel budgets, cutting equipment and supply budgets, eliminating open positions, and leaving vacant positions of departing faculty and administrative staff.

Specifically, more than twice as many public universities in this sample had enrollment increases from fall 1990 to fall 1991 as had decreases. For those with declines, half were planned, half unexpected. Public tuition rates rose as fast as the prior year or faster at two-thirds of the schools. State appropriations were higher than in prior years at half the institutions but were sharply cut back at the other half. These changes were similar to those experienced in 1991–1992, except that state support cuts were much more common in 1991–1992.

Table 1.1. Survey Response Rates by Institutional Type

Institution Type	Number of Responses	Number of Institutions	Rate (in %)
Public universities	36	56	64
Private research and doctoral	16	35	46
Private comprehensive	12	16	75
Private liberal arts and others	61	81	75
Total	125	188	66

Source: Based on Dunn, 1991b.

Despite concerns about demographics, enrollments were up as often as down among the private research, doctoral, and comprehensive universities. They rose at nineteen liberal arts colleges but fell at twenty-seven others. Shortfalls, where they occurred, were generally unanticipated. Tuition rates rose at all of these institutions, but for most the increase from FY91 to FY92 was less than it had been the prior year. Many of these private schools also reported sharply reduced state support for scholarships and other programs. These changes continued the trends identified one year ago.

As summarized in Table 1.2, many of these public and private institutions reported continuing or instituting cost containment measures in FY92. As with FY91, the most frequent options were freezing nonpersonnel budgets and cutting equipment and supply budgets. The measures of postponing plant maintenance and renovations and centralizing equipment purchases were less frequent than in FY91. A few more schools than in FY91 were able to vacate space. The number of schools cutting benefits or requiring additional employee contributions was about the same as FY91, but the number adding to benefit programs fell to less than a third of the 1991 level.

Despite changes in enrollments, the numbers of executive, managerial, and other nonfaculty personnel held steady at most of these public universities, with a few up and a few down (see Table 1.3). About half the institutions gave normal salary increases, but the rest reported frozen salaries. In FY91, most had increased staff and had given normal salary increases. Among private institutions, the number cutting administrative staff slightly surpassed the number increasing it, and most institutions gave normal salary increases. These changes closely paralleled FY91.

In general, institutions cut "other nonfaculty" personnel somewhat more frequently than they cut executives and managers. Reductions mainly took the form of nonreplacement of departing personnel, seldom layoffs, and they affected full-time personnel more often than part time.

As in FY91, and despite the reality or imminence of a squeeze on resources, most of these institutions increased their faculty numbers or held them steady, and almost all gave reasonable salary increases (see Table 1.4). Some public institutions froze salaries. Where reductions were necessary, departing faculty were not replaced, open positions were eliminated, and non–tenure eligible faculty were cut. In 1991, most cuts were of part-timers, but, in 1992, full-time faculty were affected as well. Where programs were added, faculty were as apt to be newly hired as transferred from other programs. Only one or two institutions reported cutting programs.

Only twelve of these institutions (four public, two private research and doctoral, three private comprehensive, and three private liberal arts) had begun formal Total Quality Management programs. This number is up from eight in 1991 but cannot be said to represent a trend. Most had

Table 1.2. Institutional Cost Containment Measures in Fiscal Year 1992

Institution Type	Cut Travel	Cut Membership	Cut Supplies	Cut Equipment	Hold Expenses	Centralized Travel	Centralized Equipment
Public universities	9	8	9	9	8	1	3
Private research and doctoral	4	2	4	6	8	2	3
Private comprehensive	2	4	5	4	5	0	2
Private liberal arts and others	11	12	19	21	30	4	11

Institution Type	Cut Library	Vacate Space	Reduced Maintenance	Added Benefits	Cut Benefits	Increased Employee Contribution
Public universities	5	2	5	6	6	14
Private research and doctoral	3	2	5	6	2	4
Private comprehensive	2	0	4	3	0	1
Private liberal arts and others	7	4	8	6	4	16

Note: Table figures are the number of institutional respondents to 1991 survey conducted by the Center for Planning Information, Tufts University. Public universities, $N = 36$; private research and doctoral, $N = 16$; private comprehensive, $N = 12$; and private liberal arts and others, $N = 61$.

Source: Based on Dunn, 1991b.

Table 1.3. Nonfaculty Personnel Profiles and Cost Containment Measures in Fiscal Year 1992

	Executive and Managerial Personnel						
	Up 4%+	Up 2–4%	Up 0–2%	Even	Down 0–2%	Down 2–4%	Down 4%+
Public universities	3	2	4	17	3	3	2
Private research and doctoral	1	0	6	3	6	2	1
Private comprehensive	0	0	3	5	4	0	0
Private liberal arts and others	1	3	8	29	9	3	4

	Personnel Reduction Policies		
	Non-replacement	Layoff	Other
Public universities	5	4	2
Private research and doctoral	8	4	3
Private comprehensive	4	0	0
Private liberal arts and others	13	2	3

Other Nonfaculty Staff

	Up 4%+	Up 2–4%	Up 0–2%	Even	Down 0–2%	Down 2–4%	Down 4%+
Public universities	6	3	3	13	6	1	2
Private research and doctoral	0	1	4	4	6	3	1
Private comprehensive	1	0	3	4	3	0	1
Private liberal arts and others	1	1	10	22	14	2	5

Personnel Reduction Policies / **Personnel Affected**

	Non-replacement	Layoff	Other	Full Time	Part Time
Public universities	11	4	1	9	4
Private research and doctoral	9	6	1	7	4
Private comprehensive	5	2	0	2	1
Private liberal arts and others	20	5	4	16	4

Administrative Salaries

	Up 4%+	Up 2–4%	Up 0–2%	Even	Down 0–2%	Down 2–4%	Down 4%+
Public universities	8	8	4	14	1	0	0
Private research and doctoral	6	4	1	4	1	0	0
Private comprehensive	8	2	1	1	0	0	0
Private liberal arts and others	40	10	0	3	4	0	2

Note: Table figures are the number of institutional respondents to 1991 survey conducted by the Center for Planning Information, Tufts University. Public universities, N = 36; private research and doctoral, N = 16; private comprehensive, N = 12; and private liberal arts and others, N = 61.

Source: Based on Dunn, 1991b.

Table 1.4. Faculty Profiles and Cost Containment Measures in Fiscal Year 1992

	Number of Faculty						
	Up 4%+	Up 2–4%	Up 0–2%	Even	Down 0–2%	Down 2–4%	Down 4%+
Public universities	3	7	10	8	4	0	2
Private research and doctoral	1	1	5	3	4	1	0
Private comprehensive	2	1	2	3	2	0	1
Private liberal arts and others	2	4	18	23	9	1	0

	Faculty Reduction Policies		
	Non-replacement	Program Cuts	Other
Public universities	7	1	0
Private research and doctoral	3	0	0
Private comprehensive	2	0	0
Private liberal arts and others	10	0	0

Faculty Affected

	Tenured	Tenure Track	Non-Tenure Eligible	Open Positions	Full Time	Part Time
Public universities	0	1	5	7	3	5
Private research and doctoral	1	2	3	4	2	2
Private comprehensive	1	2	2	0	3	2
Private liberal arts and others	1	2	4	3	6	4

	Program Cuts		Program Adds	
	Layoff	Transfers Out	New Hires	Transfers In
Public universities	0	0	3	7
Private research and doctoral	1	1	2	1
Private comprehensive	0	0	3	1
Private liberal arts and others	0	0	4	2

Faculty Salaries

	Up 4%+	Up 2–4%	Up 0–2%	Even	Down 0–2%	Down 2–4%	Down 4%+
Public universities	10	9	5	11	0	0	0
Private research and doctoral	11	2	0	2	0	0	0
Private comprehensive	8	3	0	1	0	0	0
Private liberal arts and others	48	4	1	3	5	0	0

Note: Table figures are the number of institutional respondents to 1991 survey conducted by the Center for Planning Information, Tufts University. Public universities, $N = 36$; private research and doctoral, $N = 16$; private comprehensive, $N = 12$; and private liberal arts and others, $N = 61$.

Source: Based on Dunn, 1991b.

not adopted Total Quality Management or did not recognize the concept by that name.

Other steps taken to contain expenditures included productivity analyses of administrative and academic activities, strategic planning exercises, review of publications, work simplification studies, setting of targets for cost reduction and service improvement, contracting out, and general frugality.

Predictions and Envoi

The survey results illustrate the impact of budget shortfalls on the day-to-day operations of institutions of higher learning. As pointed out earlier, the acid test for decision makers is to keep the urgent and the important in proper perspective. If we have allowed the urgent to crowd out the important in the recent past, what can we do about it in the future? I am not optimistic. Several predictions seem reasonable.

First, pressures to keep college costs down are pervasive, recalcitrant, beyond the institutions' ability to control, and likely to be with us for some time: (1) shrinkage in the traditional populations that many of these institutions serve and changes in preparation and in aspirations among growing parts of the population; (2) constraints on clients' ability to pay, related to national productivity problems; state and federal budget woes, based on depressed economies and lack of national competitiveness; and (3) devaluation of public esteem for higher education, especially in view of growing consensus on other social needs such as health care, K–12 education, homelessness, and crime control.

Second, colleges and universities will have to accommodate their own idea-factory needs by what Zemsky and Massy (1990) refer to as "growth by substitution." This kind of growth is difficult to achieve because some parts of a college's cost structure (existing plant, tenured faculty) are hard to change, but it is possible.

Third, the built-in economics of the industry—the first cost increase factor—will not change. Faculty salaries will rise even faster as colleges compete to replace large numbers of retirees. To the extent that colleges cannot pass on these increased costs, they will have to absorb them by eliminating marginal programs and cutting staff and activities in other areas.

To date, most of the institutions responding to the survey reported here have made marginal and reluctant responses. Most have cut supplies and equipment, a few have begun to trim administrative staff and fringe benefits, most continue normal salary increases, virtually none has cut academic programs, and many are increasing faculty numbers!

In FY91, most of these institutions were scrambling to make cuts to take effect one year later. While there have been changes, nothing major seems to have happened yet. Few schools apparently view the situation as a multiyear squeeze requiring serious review of the institutions' "product line"—or if they do, the results of their decisions are not yet evident.

In a competitive environment, it is understandable that individual institutions believe that they will do better by strengthening their offerings than by pruning them and reducing their cost of delivery. They should do the former, but they will have to do the latter as well.

Will costs be constrained? Yes. Colleges and universities in most areas of the country simply cannot get all of the funds that they think they will need. We face more difficult external competitive pressures as prospective students have more choices and want to negotiate prices with us. And we are all much more sensitive to appearances, having been publically whipped for alleged price collusion, research fraud, athletic overindulgences, and overbilling for indirect costs. Our boards of trustees or regents can help us keep our eyes on the long-term goals and on our relationships to the society of which we are a part; but they too can succumb to our articulate advocacy of some urgent internal need—or to their own drives for prestige for the institutions that they defend.

This is a pessimistic view from an optimistic person. (No one should be in education who is not an optimist at heart.) Most colleges and universities will survive into the next century with strong and valuable programs, having found many new ways to accomplish what they need to do. I just think that they will be thinner.

So, for a time, we shall have our eyes open to the external world and focused on the important as well as the urgent. Let's hope that we can keep them open.

References

Bowen, H. R. *The Costs of Higher Education: How Much Do Colleges and Universities Spend Per Student and How Much Should They Spend?* San Francisco: Jossey-Bass, 1980.

Dunn, J. A., Jr. "How Colleges Should Handle Their Endowment." *Planning for Higher Education,* 1991a, *19* (3), 32–37.

Dunn, J. A., Jr. *Results of a Quick Survey on Cost Containment and Downsizing.* Medford, Mass.: Center for Planning Information, Tufts University, 1991b.

Dunn, J. A., Jr. *Trends in Student Charges, 1987–88 Through 1991–92.* HEDS Report 91-6. Medford, Mass.: Higher Education Data Sharing Consortium, Tufts University, 1991c.

Frances, C., and Williamson, P. "Study of the Factors Underlying Endowment Growth." Unpublished manuscript, Carol Frances and Associates, 1992.

Middaugh, M. F., and Hollowell, D. E. "Strategies for Cost Containment at a Medium-Sized Research University." Paper presented at the annual meeting of the Society for College and University Planning, Seattle, Washington, July 14–17, 1991.

Zemsky, R., and Massy, W. F. "Cost Containment: Committing to a New Economic Reality." *Change,* 1990, *22* (6), 16–22.

JOHN A. DUNN, JR., is president of Dean Junior College, Franklin, Massachusetts, and is past executive director of the Center for Planning Information, a tax-exempt, not-for-profit organization that supports college and university planning, at Tufts University, Medford, Massachusetts.

A multitude of cost factors in higher education is cause for dismay and reason for hope.

Factors That Influence Costs in Higher Education

Paul T. Brinkman

No absolute framework exists for determining that higher education costs are too high, too low, or about right. But concern about these costs by vital constituencies and an obligation to use resources efficiently are reasons enough to seek ways to contain costs. That search rightly begins with an assessment of the factors that affect these costs. This has been done before in a variety of ways: for example, W. Bowen (1968), Verry and Davies (1976), Robinson, Ray, and Turk (1977), H. Bowen (1980), Massy (1990), Simpson (1991), and Halstead (1991). The present chapter builds on an earlier effort to develop a comprehensive outline for delineating and categorizing influences on the costs of higher education (Brinkman, 1988).

Overview

Two types of cost are at issue: total cost of production and average cost per unit of output. Production costs incurred by colleges and universities are a function of the quantity of resources (or inputs) used in the production process and the prices paid for those resources. Thus, the task is to describe the various cost factors that influence either the amount or the type of resources used and the prices of those resources.

For organizational purposes, those factors can be located within one of three primary sources: (1) individual colleges and universities, (2) the higher education community, and (3) the broad socioeconomic and scientific-technological environment. Within each source, influences on cost can be viewed as the result of either culture or material conditions (see Figure 2.1). The desired contrast, in other words, is between what people value, believe, desire, and so on (as part of various collectivities) and the actual state of affairs or conditions in which they work. Some of

NEW DIRECTIONS FOR INSTITUTIONAL RESEARCH, no. 75, Fall 1992 © Jossey-Bass Publishers

the boundaries may be difficult to draw and should be taken as suggestive only. Moreover, the many second-order effects stemming from the
interaction between the cultural and the material are largely ignored
here.

Cost Factors That Operate Within Institutions

Differences in costs per student among comparable institutions demonstrate that cost factors operating within institutions are potent. Such
factors are certainly the most immediate causes of higher education
resource requirements.

Culture. Costs at a particular college or university are affected by
that institution's culture, that is, its shared values, beliefs, norms, attitudes, and self-image.

Goals and Purposes. The service mentality that is imbedded in the
very concept of "community college" is an example of a broad purpose
with significant cost implications. Another example is the special requirements of the commitment to being a research university.

Valued Attributes. Many valued attributes might affect costs, such as
being a "caring" institution versus one that is concerned about being
efficient. A critical attribute in this regard is the extent of commitment to
quality. For example, think of the long-term cost consequences of "de-
cent" versus "world class" as the leitmotif of a chemistry department.

Material Conditions. Material conditions within a college or university, such as the services provided, are among the most obvious cost
factors.

Services. Three types of cost factors are involved on the production
side: the services themselves, technical relationships among inputs and

Figure 2.1. Factors
Influencing Costs in Higher Education

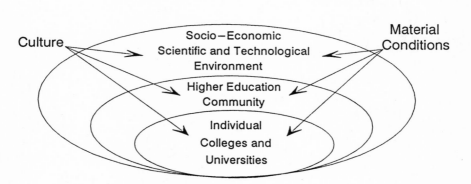

outputs, and the price of inputs. Higher education produces three types of basic services—instruction, research, and public service. Not much is known about the ideal mix of these three from a cost perspective. Cohn, Rhine, and Santos (1989) found evidence of economies of scope for the combination of instruction and research, that is, it is less expensive to produce them jointly than separately.

The mix of services within instruction ranges from the very narrow to the extremely broad, depending on the institution. From a cost perspective, these services can be portrayed as a matrix with degree programs along one axis and levels of instruction along the other. The cost impact of higher levels of instruction is fairly consistent: The higher the level of instruction, the higher the cost per student credit hour (for some estimates of these differences, see Brinkman, 1989).

Costs per student credit hour vary widely by discipline or field owing to differences in the quantity, type, and prices of the inputs required (faculty, equipment, supplies, and so on) and their utilization (for example, student-faculty ratios). The number of disciplines and fields in which degrees are awarded, holding enrollment constant, may affect average costs (Brinkman, 1981). The structure of the curriculum also affects cost; Massy (1990) argues that the typical, semistructured approach is more costly than either a highly structured curriculum or a totally unstructured curriculum.

Costs for support services are partly dependent on the basic services offered. For example, accounting at a research university will normally include a sizable contracts and grants division. The composition of the revenue stream also makes a difference; for example, private institutions have little choice but to devote major resources to fund-raising. The extent of some support services, such as health care and security, are impacted by local circumstances.

Little is known about the effect of size on the cost of research and public service activities, although Cohn, Rhine, and Santos (1989) found evidence of positive returns to scale for research. Scale economies occur in instruction, but the effects are not large except at the low end of the enrollment range; scale economies are more readily apparent in the support areas (Brinkman and Leslie, 1986). It is usually inappropriate to take scale-related findings at face value, as those findings can be affected by policy choices and recent changes in size (a phenomenon explored at length in Metz and Siegfried, 1991).

Assets. The condition of an institution's assets affects its costs. Consider, for example, the likely difference in production costs between two institutions that provide virtually identical services but do so using physical plants that differ greatly in age or prior maintenance.

The bulk of the operating budget goes to paying for staff salaries and benefits; thus, an institution's costs are influenced by the characteristics of its work force. Age, experience, training, track record, gender, and ethnicity can impact on productivity or salary level and thus on costs.

Physical Environment. Institutions face different costs depending on their locations. Climatic and other natural conditions constitute one dimension, affecting the cost of utilities, snow removal, and so on. The other dimension consists of man-made structures such as urban centers or transportation links. For example, campus security costs and unit labor costs are likely to be considerably greater for institutions in large cities than for comparable institutions in rural areas.

Structures, Policies, and Processes for Governance and Management. Budget-related incentives, such as the treatment of unspent balances and budget overruns, are a good example of how management policies affect costs. The impact of such incentives is discussed at length in Hoenack and Berg (1980).

Budgetary and other financial controls obviously affect costs. An institution's knowledge of its own costs could also have an impact, and that information is itself costly. Hoenack (1983) provides the best discussion of the trade-offs involved.

There are other ways in which governance and management can affect costs. For example, institutions are likely to incur otherwise avoidable costs if they address problems by hiring additional people instead of creating new policies, maintain duplicative structures and functions, and never even look for ways to trim costs.

Revenues. Cost variations among institutions are sometimes due to variations in revenue. For example, institutions with more revenue, other things being equal, can afford to deploy a richer mix of resources, such as higher salaries and lower student-staff ratios, and are likely to do so (H. Bowen, 1980). Another revenue-related effect is the cost of raising revenues, from operating a development office to writing grant proposals, to recruiting students.

Cost Factors Within the Higher Education Community

The higher education community consists of colleges and universities, other organizations and associations related to higher education, and, in varying degrees, all of the individuals who work in academia. Membership has important ramifications for cost because of various community-based attitudes and expectations as well as material conditions in the community.

Culture. Most of the cost-related concepts that have been popularized recently—output creep, academic ratchet, growth force, and administrative lattice—along with older notions, such as the cost disease, can best be thought of as community matters. While the phenomena to which these and other community concepts refer are realized only in individual institutions, the phenomena are widespread and not unique to a given institution.

Faculty Norms. Faculty attitudes and expectations are shaped and nurtured in a system dominated by inbreeding. Especially critical are expectations about work load (number of classes, class sizes, time for research and other creative activities, and so on) and work content (what is worth doing, how it should be done, and the basis for evaluating performance).

These expectations have been changing in some segments of the community. James (1978) found, for example, that during the period from the early 1960s to the mid-1970s, the effort devoted to teaching at research universities dropped from around 70 percent of the time used for professional activities to somewhat less than 50 percent. The time devoted to research increased from less than 20 percent to about 30 percent. Massy (1990) refers to this change as an example of output creep, reflecting its long-term, gradual, and unplanned nature. Because these changes tend to go in one direction only, the analogy of a ratchet has been invoked. As Zemsky (1990, p. 5) puts it, "Each turn of the ratchet has drawn the norm of faculty activity away from institutionally defined goals and toward the more specialized concerns of faculty research, publication, professional service, and personal pursuits."

While the ratchet is much in evidence at research universities, it is less so at other four-year institutions, and hardly at all at community colleges. Even at research universities the faculty preference for research is no greater than what they perceive to be their institution's preference for research (Blackburn, Bieber, Lawrence, and Trautvetter, 1991).

Faculty expectations regarding appropriate activity vary not only by institution type but also by discipline. The influence of the discipline represents a combination of habits of thought and technical relationships of production. The latter belong under material conditions. The former belong here, as cultural phenomena, and are partly responsible for differences in average costs among the disciplines. The combined effects of discipline and institutional type on faculty norms are explored at length by Clark (1987). Alpert (1985) examines the relationships between campus and disciplinary interests and the implications for costs.

Finally, it is the nature of faculty to be thinking of new things to do, such as offering new courses and new programs. Massy (1990) refers to this as the "growth force." This vitality, as he points out, is needed, but it puts a constant upward pressure on costs. As indicated below, the internal growth force is complemented by societal expectations for enhanced higher education services, the growth ethic inherent to capitalism, and the dynamism of modern science and technology.

Administrator Norms. Administrators also have norms, again because of inbreeding and an external labor market that tends to reward certain types of performance (James, 1990). Some of the norms lead to higher costs. For example, a collegial approach to management is time consuming and resource intensive and it may, according to Zemsky (1990), engender a lack of decisiveness that is not conducive to cost containment. He also mentions a form of entrepreneurship in which successful administrative units have a tendency to take on additional responsibilities. As these units grow, they establish additional relationships with one another; thus the metaphor of the administrative "lattice."

Institutional Norms. The quest for prestige, which is likely to have cost implications, is common among higher education institutions, especially universities (Breneman, 1970; H. Bowen, 1980; Garvin, 1980). Indeed, in a recent study, reputation is used as the sole output for prestigious research universities (McGuire, Richman, Daly, and Jorjani, 1988). Similarly, few institutions can resist the "bigger is better" syndrome, although institutions define it differently.

Competition in also normative (O'Keefe, 1987). In higher education, it tends to drive up costs. The effects can be seen in bidding wars for faculty stars, efforts to climb higher education's hierarchical structure, the proliferation of student services, the "me too" syndrome in which whatever one institution gets (in a system), the others must have as well; and even the "peer" approach to funding requests, given that it tends to be pursued primarily by those who have something to gain from it. Price competition, which constrains costs in other economic sectors, is only moderately effective in higher education.

Efficiency, by contrast, is not normative in the community of institutions. It is not a compelling notion except under conditions of duress, and even then its value is instrumental (a tool for survival) rather than intrinsic. Striving to be efficient is not the same as being fiscally conservative. The latter normally means keeping expenditures in line with revenues and does not in itself reduce the impetus to increase revenues.

According to H. Bowen (1980), cost per student is dependent on the revenue available and not the technical requirements of production. He goes on to claim that institutions spend all that they receive in revenues. It happens, however, that many colleges and universities, in both sectors, do not spend all of their revenues in any given year, or even over a number of years. Nor is it true universally, as he claims, that higher education institutions are revenue maximizers. This may be due, in part, to incompetence, but the motives of higher education officials are more complex than Bowen's presentation would allow.

Nonetheless, there is much truth in the revenue explanation for costs—in a normative sense. To the extent that the revenue explanation is true, anything that affects revenue affects costs.

Agency Norms. Agencies such as accreditation bodies and coordinating boards have norms too. These norms are strongly influenced by higher education institutions, but they are also influenced by professional organizations, state legislatures, and so on. They affect higher education costs through agency regulations; Thompson and Zumeta (1981) examine this connection.

Material Conditions. Material conditions vary in the extent that they are clearly within, or of, the higher education community. For example, the condition of the science disciplines is clearly of interest but cannot easily be separated from the broader environment.

Structure of the Community. Some of the structural cost factors include the presence of a large private sector, an enormous number of institutions, numerous interest groups, and various agencies, such as accreditation bodies and coordinating boards, that have authority to promulgate regulations.

Condition of the Disciplines. The condition of each of the disciplines has important consequences for the cost of providing instructional and research services. At issue is the way knowledge is gained, what is known, the structure of that knowledge, and its rate of growth.

Production Technologies. Production technologies have a direct and immediate impact on costs. Their impact is a function of both their inherent characteristics and cultural acceptance.

It has been argued that higher education unavoidably experiences rising costs in real terms because the rest of the economy is gradually becoming more productive while higher education's productivity remains constant. This phenomenon, referred to as the "cost disease," is sometimes illustrated by analogy with the productivity problem facing a string quartet, which cannot improve its efficiency by reducing personnel.

The illustration has force, however, only from the limited perspective wherein productivity refers to the act of producing a particular piece of music at a particular time and place. From a broader perspective, a string quartet has more opportunities to increase its productivity than does, for example, a company that makes automobiles. For example, through one "production" the quartet can provide music for many thousands of people through a radio broadcast. Similarly, information technology may eventually provide a way out of the cost disease in higher education, if we will let it. Productivity gains from that source will be limited, for instance, by the view that learning occurs only when student and teacher are together in a classroom.

Labor Markets. The higher education labor market is inextricably linked to the larger economy. Faculty constitute the segment that is most clearly a community labor market. Market characteristics vary greatly by discipline and institutional type, with considerable impact on faculty salaries. The labor market has the potential to exert extreme pressure on production costs, as the recent experience with salaries in some business and engineering disciplines has demonstrated.

Cost Factors That Operate Within Society at Large

Higher education institutions and the higher education community exist within a complex environment. Social movements, technological developments, economic changes, and so on push and pull on higher education and affect its costs in many ways.

Culture. Some of the cultural dimensions involve higher education directly. In other instances, the effects are indirect.

Expectations Regarding Higher Education. Higher education has had to respond to a continuing increase in demand for more types of services for more segments of society. It is expected to find room for anyone who wants to enroll. It is expected to take students even if they are not prepared for college. It is expected, by and large, to let students study in whatever fields they choose, and to offer programs of interest regardless of cost. It is expected to be available wherever there are people, however few. All of these expectations affect costs.

Valuing Higher Education. Society's overall investment in higher education reflects its value to society. The total cost of higher education would be less if society valued it less. Parents and students are said to perceive tuition levels as indicative of quality, at least within the private sector (Werth, 1988). Their judgment may be well founded in a general way (Gilmore, 1990). Their willingness to pay higher prices, however, makes higher levels of institutional expenditures possible if not probable.

Localities value colleges and universities for their local economic and cultural contributions. This can lead, through the political process, to the construction of more institutions than might otherwise be needed. The same valuation makes it difficult to close institutions regardless of their relative inefficiency.

Society. In a capitalist society, the prevailing belief is that growth and competitiveness are essential. Even if higher education became less competitive, it would still face a highly competitive, rapidly changing environment.

Social movements, in the sense of basic changes in attitudes and expectations, continually impact on higher education costs. They exert influence by changing higher education's client base, the services it renders, and the composition of its resources.

Material Conditions. The broad material environment within which colleges and universities operate is multifaceted, complex, and evolving. Only a few of its many impacts on costs can be discussed here.

Government/Politics. The impact on costs of government intrusion in higher education has often been noted. Not only do institutions use resources in meeting government regulations, but they also consume resources in providing compliance information.

Government action directly affects costs in higher education through the revenue effect. For example, relatively low levels of state appropriations combined with legislative controls on tuition increases are likely to result in relatively low expenditures by the public institutions involved. The funding mechanisms used by states may affect costs too, depending on the incentives contained therein (for example, rewarding increased enrollment).

State systems may be more costly than student demand would require because of political agendas. Institutions may meet outside political opposition when attempting to cut programs.

The judicial branch of government impacts on costs not only through specific rulings but in the more general way that it locates higher education on the legal map. Higher education costs vary directly with the degree to which colleges and universities are open to suit.

Economy. The price of goods and services in the economy has an immediate impact on costs. Another vector of economic influence is indirect, through revenues. The impact of state economies on the public sector is well known; the national and global economies are factors too (Anderson and Myerson, 1990). A growing economy is likely accompanied by higher costs. A bad economy brings with it the constraint of the "revenue diet."

Demographics. The overall number of persons eligible for college can affect costs. Given a constant participation rate, a larger pool of students will lead to higher total costs.

The composition of the population influences costs too. Arguably, the more homogeneous the population to be served, the lower the average cost per student. The composition of the relevant population has changed in the past few decades. With respect to women, this is due to changes in attitudes about who ought to go to college. In the case of minorities, both attitudes and demographic changes have been important.

The geographical distribution of people also affects costs. This is especially obvious in the sparsely populated states.

Science and Technology. Almost anywhere one looks on the campus, the cost effects of science and technology are visible: fiber-optic cables, science laboratories, writing laboratories, offices with computers instead of typewriters, deans cobbling together the enormous sums required to equip a new experimentalist, and disciplines that did not even exist a generation or two ago.

Of all of the cost factors mentioned in this chapter, science and technology are perhaps the most threatening in their continuing demand for new resources. Yet, they offer promise as a way out of higher education's productivity-based, long-run, upward cost spiral. One way or another, it is clear that higher education's ability to deal with this challenge will be an important element in its long-run cost picture.

Social Structures and Processes. Changes in social structures can have long-term effects on costs. One of the most fundamental developments during the past century has been the increasing prevalence of organizations that can operate effectively only with the help of large numbers of college-educated individuals. This development has contributed to the manyfold increase in enrollments and thus to total cost.

A litigious society is an expensive society within which to operate a college or university. It would be surprising indeed to find a college or university that was not spending far more today for legal services than even just a decade ago.

Implications for Cost Containment

Effective cost containment strategies will be based on a sound appraisal of the factors that influence cost. This chapter was designed to underscore the complexity of the situation.

If we are concerned about costs, it is worth pondering how we think about our institutions and what sort of social constructs we foster, starting with our most fundamental assumptions about purpose, the relative value of alternative activities, work load, and acceptable technologies. To use the current jargon, we need to deconstruct those assumptions, that is, show them for what they are. It may take a crisis to allow this to happen, but perhaps just candid discourse will help.

The objective functions that promote the academic ratchet, the administrative lattice, the overemphasis on competition, and so on cannot readily be addressed at the local, or single institution, level under present circumstances. Yet, individual institutions must take leadership positions to move the community toward norms that are more conducive to efficiency. Incentive systems need to be examined carefully. Institutions ought to set targets for productivity enhancements and develop more effective strategies for budgeting.

Higher education must try to take better advantage of the technology that it is helping to create. To have any chance of overcoming the cost disease, we shall have to move away from the concept of instruction as inextricably linked to hours in class. So doing will free us to make the most of the new technologies.

More emphasis needs to be put on cooperation, less on competition. Again, technology may help, as it is making possible new ways to share resources. Investment costs are sure to be substantial, but some development costs could be shared.

There is a basis for optimism. The extent of the variation in costs among similar institutions suggests that some institutions have figured out how to contain costs, at least relatively speaking. Perhaps a reversal of form is in order. Maybe the less affluent institutions ought to become the models.

References

Alpert, D. "Performance and Paralysis: The Organizational Context of the American Research University." *Journal of Higher Education,* 1985, *56,* 241–281.

Anderson, R. E., and Myerson, J. W. (eds.). *Financial Planning Under Economic Uncertainty.* New Directions for Higher Education, no. 69. San Francisco: Jossey-Bass, 1990.

Blackburn, R. T., Bieber, J. P., Lawrence, J. H., and Trautvetter, L. "Faculty at Work: Focus on Research, Scholarship, and Service." *Research in Higher Education,* 1991, *32* (4), 386–415.

Bowen, H. R. *The Costs of Higher Education: How Much Do Colleges and Universities Spend Per Student and How Much Should They Spend?* San Francisco: Jossey-Bass, 1980.

Bowen, W. G. *The Economics of the Major Private Universities.* Berkeley, Calif.: Carnegie Commission on Higher Education, 1968.

Breneman, D. *An Economic Theory of Ph.D. Production: The Case at Berkeley.* Berkeley, Calif.: Ford Foundation Program for Research in University Administration, University of California, 1970.

Brinkman, P. T. "Factors Affecting Instructional Costs at Major Research Universities." *Journal of Higher Education,* 1981, *52* (3), 265–279.

Brinkman, P. T. *The Cost of Providing Higher Education: A Conceptual Overview.* Denver, Colo.: State Higher Education Executive Officers, 1988.

Brinkman, P. T. "Instructional Costs Per Student Credit Hour: Differences by Level of Instruction." *Journal of Education Finance,* 1989, *15,* 34–52.

Brinkman, P. T., and Leslie, L. L. "Economies of Scale in Higher Education: Sixty Years of Research." *Review of Higher Education,* 1986, *10* (1), 1–28.

Clark, B. R. *The Academic Life: Small Worlds, Different Worlds.* Princeton, N.J.: Carnegie Foundation for the Advancement of Teaching, 1987.

Cohn, E., Rhine, S.L.W., and Santos, M. C. "Institutions of Higher Education as Multi-Product Firms: Economies of Scale and Scope." *Review of Economics and Statistics,* 1989, *71,* 284–290.

Garvin, D. *The Economics of University Behavior.* San Diego, Calif.: Academic Press, 1980.

Gilmore, J. L. *Price and Quality in Higher Education.* Washington, D.C.: Government Printing Office, 1990.

Halstead, K. *Higher Education Revenues and Expenditures: A Study of Institutional Costs.* Washington, D.C.: Research Associates of Washington, 1991.

Hoenack, S. A. *Economic Behavior Within Organizations.* New York: Cambridge University Press, 1983.

Hoenack, S. A., and Berg, D. J. "The Roles of Incentives in Academic Planning." In R. B. Heydinger (ed.), *Academic Planning for the 1980s.* New Directions for Institutional Research, no. 28. San Francisco: Jossey-Bass, 1980.

James, E. "Product Mix and Cost Disaggregation: A Reinterpretation of the Economics of Higher Education." *Journal of Human Resources,* 1978, *13,* 157–186.

James, E. "Decision Processes and Priorities in Higher Education." In S. A. Hoenack and E. L. Collins (eds.), *The Economics of American Universities.* Albany: State University of New York Press, 1990.

McGuire, J. W., Richman, M. L., Daly, R. F., and Jorjani, S. "The Efficient Production of 'Reputation' by Prestige Research Universities in the United States." *Journal of Higher Education,* 1988, *59* (4), 365–389.

Massy, W. F. "The Dynamics of Academic Productivity." In W. F. Massy and R. Zemsky, *The Dynamics of Academic Productivity*. (J. R. Mingle, comp.) Denver, Colo.: State Higher Education Executive Officers, 1990.

Metz, G., and Siegfried, J. J. "Costs and Productivity in American Colleges and Universities." In C. T. Clotfelter, R. G. Ehrenberg, M. Getz, and J. J. Siegfried (eds.), *Economic Challenges in Higher Education*. Chicago: University of Chicago Press, 1991.

O'Keefe, M. "Where Does the Money Really Go?" *Change*, 1987, *19* (6), 12–34.

Robinson, D. D., Ray, H. W., and Turk, F. J. "Cost Behavior Analysis for Planning in Higher Education." *NACUBO Professional File*, 1977, *9*, 1–51.

Simpson, W. B. *Cost Containment for Higher Education: Strategies for Public Policy and Institutional Administration*. New York: Praeger, 1991.

Thompson, F., and Zumeta, W. "A Regulatory Model of Governmental Coordinating Activities in the Higher Education Sector." *Economics of Education Review*, 1981, *1* (1), 27–52.

Verry, D., and Davies, B. *University Costs and Outputs*. Amsterdam, The Netherlands: Elsevier, 1976.

Werth, B. "Why Is College So Expensive? Maybe America Wants It That Way." *Change*, 1988, *20* (2), 13–25.

Zemsky, R. "The Lattice and the Ratchet." *Policy Perspectives*, 1990, *2* (4), 1–8.

PAUL T. BRINKMAN is director of Planning and Policy Studies at the University of Utah, Salt Lake City.

Evaluation of academic productivity is a complex undertaking and often a taboo subject in higher education. The authors investigate factors that increase or restrict academic productivity through a review of recent studies and their own empirical research.

Evaluating Academic Productivity and Quality

Jeffrey L. Gilmore, Duc-Le To

Cost disease, growth force, organizational slack, output creep, ratchet mechanism, add-on spiral, and cost-plus pricing—these concepts and theories provide a rich vocabulary for conceptualizing and confronting the critical issue of academic productivity. Yet, as one leading theorist on the subject points out, academic productivity "has long been a taboo subject in American higher education" as evidenced by a "dearth of scholarship on the subject" (Massy, 1991, p. 1).

What do we know about academic productivity? How can we define and measure it? What do recent studies tell us about how to improve it? What empirical evidence is available to guide our understanding of why some institutions are more productive than others? This chapter addresses these questions by presenting an overview of productivity concepts, by exploring several studies of institutional productivity, and by presenting the results of two recent research projects that attempt to identify the factors underlying academic quality and faculty productivity.

Conceptualizing and Measuring Productivity

A study of organizational productivity involves measuring institutional output per unit of input. Productivity can be increased by producing

We thank Thomas J. Calhoun, a graduate intern from the University of Chicago, and Mindi S. Barth, an education program specialist at the U.S. Department of Education, for their research support of this project. This chapter is intended to promote the exchange of ideas among researchers and policymakers. The views are those of the authors, and no official support by the U.S. Department of Education is intended or should be inferred.

more outputs with the same inputs, or by producing the same outputs with fewer inputs. Although productivity is usually defined in terms of the output of goods or services per hour of labor, in a broader sense productivity encompasses not only the quantity of outputs but also an element of quality. That is, a gain in the number of outputs per unit of input would not represent an increase in productivity if, at the same time, the quality of the outputs decreased.

Productivity studies most often use mathematical methods to examine the relationships between institutional resources and outcomes. Such studies are based on economic theories of the firm, particularly production theory and cost theory. Analyses of productivity based on production theory are usually done through the specification and testing of production function models (for a thorough review of these studies, see Schapiro, 1987), whereas studies based on cost theory typically use unit-cost analysis such as costs per student, per credit, or per degree (examples of this approach include James, 1978; Bowen, 1980; and To, 1987).

The production function is intended to represent the process by which an institution transforms inputs into outputs. In order to specify the function precisely, a researcher must be able to identify and quantify all relevant inputs and outputs and describe their relationships in mathematical terms. Productivity studies in higher education are similar, though complicated by the fact that inputs, products, and quality are hard to define and measure.

Commonly measured resources include capital, labor, and equipment. Such inputs are relatively easy to estimate as they are most often expressed in monetary terms (for example, expenditures per student, faculty salaries, and the value of the physical plant). However, there are other equally important, but less easily defined, inputs as well. These include the personal attributes of students, faculty, and staff (such as ability, effort, energy, expertise, commitment); intangible institutional qualities (environmental synergies and organizational cultures that motivate and facilitate educational outcomes); and family and community support, encouragement, and expectations of success. All these inputs contribute to the educational enterprise.

Definition and measurement of educational outputs require careful consideration of several factors. There are three major functions of higher education—teaching, research, and public service—and each has a different set of products or outputs. Some view the outputs of education as learning in all of its manifestations, including content learning in the disciplines, the development of specific cognitive skills, and the maturation of constructive personal characteristics, behaviors, and aesthetic sensibilities. Others focus on such tangible "goods and services" as credit hours, degrees, publications, discoveries, and public contact hours.

Still others consider outputs to be synonymous with such student-centered outcomes as increased lifetime earnings, socioeconomic status, and personal life-styles and satisfaction. Obviously, many of these outputs are very difficult to measure.

Although a number of definitions of institutional quality have been advanced (Astin, 1982), the one with arguably the most credence holds that the highest quality institutions are those that effect the greatest intellectual and developmental change in their students. However, caution must be exercised here since assessment of institutional impact on student change is not the same as measurement of student outcomes. That is, a college with high student outcomes is not necessarily doing an outstanding job. If that institution has abundant resources, a distinguished faculty, and excellent students, it would be *expected* to produce above-average results. This is not the same as being highly productive. In short, colleges must "take differential recruitment into account in estimating the degree of institutional impact" (Clark and others, 1972, p. 5).

Review of Past Productivity Studies

One of the most significant studies of higher education productivity using the unit-cost approach was conducted by O'Neill (1971). Her study found no perceptible change in institutional productivity over a thirty-seven-year period as both credit hour production and total student instructional costs increased phenomenally. Skoro and Hryvniak (1980) later expanded O'Neill's methodology for an additional ten years with similar results.

Early studies of academic productivity using the production function approach failed to account for the impact of incoming student quality on institutional productivity (Knapp and Goodrich, 1952; and Knapp and Greenbaum, 1953). Holland (1957) pointed out that the "high-productivity" colleges cited by Knapp all recruited higher proportions of National Merit Scholars than did the "low-productivity" colleges.

In 1962, Astin corrected the shortcomings of earlier production function designs by comparing an institution's output rate (the proportion of students eventually obtaining Ph.D.s) with an input measure expressed in equivalent units (the *predicted* proportion of Ph.D.s), or, in other words, by defining the productivity of a college as "the ratio between its actual output and its expected output" (1962, p. 129). The major conclusion of his study was that "much of the variation among undergraduate institutions in Ph.D. output is a function of student input" (p. 131). In their extensive review of studies on college impact, Feldman and Newcomb (1969) document the differences in student characteristics and the fact that these differences vary considerably not only among students within an institution but also, and more to the point, between institutions. They emphasize that the "products" of a college (that is, educated students) must be seen in relation to their incoming character- istics. In a similar vein, an institution's other outputs should be evaluated in terms of inputs, including resources and faculty quality and time.

Other Approaches to Academic Productivity

A review of journal articles covering the past decade reveals a number of different conceptualizations for measuring academic productivity, in- cluding student outputs (Goodman, 1979; Steele, 1989), faculty contri- butions to the campus community and faculty professional development (Lincoln, 1983), and faculty members' intellectual growth (Reagan, 1985). While these writers provide useful commentary and theoretical discus- sions, they do not offer any empirical evaluations of academic productiv- ity. By far, the most common approach to academic productivity has been to measure the number of faculty publications. The results from several empirical studies have suggested that publication rates can be increased by reducing teaching loads and providing more release time for research (Schwebel, 1982; Schuttenberg, Patterson, and Sutton, 1986; Garland and Rike, 1987; Kenny, Tietjen, and Witthus, 1990; Vardan, Smulyan, Mookherjee, and Mehrotra, 1990). Although these studies suggest ways to increase faculty publications and research outputs, they all fail to take into account the allocation principle, as discussed below.

When a single input produces multiple outputs, the allocation prin- ciple becomes relevant. In a university setting, for instance, an increase in the quantity of scholarly papers due to a new program that gives faculty release time from teaching to do research does not indicate a productivity improvement. Rather, it represents a reallocation of re- sources (faculty time) from the production of one product to the produc- tion of another. The sum total of all outputs has stayed the same since the number of students taught has gone down while the number of faculty publications has increased. A rigorous study of productivity, therefore, must take into account both inputs and outputs, together with a consid- eration of the allocation principle.

A Recent Empirical Study of Academic Quality Factors

In a recent empirical study, Gilmore (1990) sought to explore the rela- tionships between college tuition charges and institutional quality, and to examine the factors underlying institutional effectiveness (defined in terms of student educational progress, a composite of freshman grade point average, sophomore retention, and graduation rates). The study used data from all of the 593 private, general baccalaureate institutions for the 1985–86 academic year and employed correlations, descriptive statistics, multiple regressions, and path analysis.

Analyses of descriptive statistics for four institutional price-by-performance groups revealed that some colleges with low endowments had high student prices but failed to deliver correspondingly high quality, services, financial aid, or student outcomes. Students at these institutions not only shouldered a greater share of their institution's total expenditures (64 percent versus 47.6 percent at more generously endowed institutions), but they also received a smaller proportion of financial aid. The aid gap (the difference between tuition charges and student assistance) for students on aid at these less endowed institutions was $2,308, compared with $1,603 for students at the low-cost, high-performance schools. In addition to the "cost burden" and the "aid gap," the less endowed institutions had other significant differences, especially in regard to their allocations of resources. They had, on average, $2.1 million more in buildings and equipment but 15 percent fewer library books and 33 percent fewer library journals.

The final empirical model developed during the study used only nine independent variables representing a combination of student and institutional characteristics. The model explained 59 percent of the variation in student educational progress, indicating that it captured the key elements underlying institutional effectiveness. Analyses of the causal model revealed that the largest effects appeared to come from institutional decisions regarding initial inputs, including decisions that set tuition levels, admissions standards, institutional size, and policies regarding at-risk students. Student ability had the strongest effect, followed closely by tuition charges and total revenues. Other significant variables were academic enrichment and student activity programs. Significant negative effects were from at-risk students and percentage of full-time faculty (this last factor was particularly strong at less selective institutions). It is surprising that faculty-student ratios were *not* a significant factor in a student's educational progress. Perhaps unmeasurable out-of-class interactions hold the key. The frequency of such interactions may not be determined by class ratios but by faculty teaching loads, dedication, and availability, suggesting that institutions could realize some cost savings by increasing class size slightly.

The results caution administrators that incoming student characteristics, affordability, and resource allocation strategies are major considerations in student academic progress, and that not all academic characteristics are beneficial for all colleges. For example, an emphasis on full-time faculty involved with research may not promote student retention and progression toward a degree, especially at institutions with underprepared or nontraditional students.

An Empirical Study of Academic Productivity

We recently completed an empirical study of academic productivity, the results of which are reported below. This new inquiry expands Gilmore's (1990) investigation by covering doctorate-granting universities and comprehensive institutions in addition to liberal arts colleges. It also analyzes academic productivity in a new way by building on Astin's (1962) earlier methodological breakthrough and using multiple-regression analyses to compare active outcomes with expected outcomes given each institution's faculty quality, student ability levels, and other resources. By accounting for the direct contributions of inputs on outputs in this manner, the study was able to focus on the institutional characteristics, processes, and environments that enhance or reduce net productivity. Student outcomes again were emphasized (as opposed to research and public service outputs) because so few studies have addressed these outputs and because there was a definite need to recast institutional effectiveness and productivity in student-centered terms.

Data. To conduct the study, data from three different sources were merged using the institutional codes of the Federal Interagency Committee on Education: (1) a special organizational survey administered by the National Association of College and University Business Officers in 1990, (2) the 1991–1992 College Board annual survey of colleges, and (3) the 1988–1989 annual Integrated Postsecondary Education Data System survey by the U.S. Department of Education. The merged data file contained information on 591 four-year institutions.

Variables. Variables used in this study can be divided into three groups: (1) two student outcome indicators, which were the dependent variables for the study; (2) a group of ten measures of student and institutional characteristics, which were used as independent variables in the multiple-regression equations to estimate expected institutional performance; and (3) a group of seventeen additional institutional factors, which were used to compare productive and underproductive institutions.

Methodology. A straightforward methodology was used to identify factors and strategies for improved productivity. First, institutions were divided by Carnegie Commission classification code into doctoral, comprehensive, and liberal arts institutions (all two-year and special institutions were excluded from the sample). Then, within each group, productive and underproductive institutions were identified. This was done in three steps. First, the ordinary least-squares method of multiple-regression analysis was used to estimate coefficients for all the variables in two predictive models of institutional productivity (see equations 1 and 2 below). Then, these regression coefficients were used with the actual variable values to calculate expected outcome scores for each institution. Last, each institution's *actual* performance (in terms of the two outcome indicators—student retention and graduation rates) was compared with its *predicted* performance (from the regression models, given its resources, student ability levels, and faculty quality). If an institution's actual performance was better than its predicted performance, it was identified as productive. If its actual outcomes were smaller than predicted, it was identified as underproductive. Finally, the profiles of the productive and underproductive institutions were analyzed by comparing their average scores (means) for each variable in the study to see if they were significantly different (by using *t*-tests). By contrasting the strategies and practices that productive versus underproductive institutions apply to their faculty, we hoped to gain a better understanding of what can be done to improve academic productivity.

Equations (1) and (2) are the independent, single-equation models used for identifying the productive and underproductive institutions for each of the two different student outcome indicators (variable definitions are provided later in the chapter).

$$
\begin{aligned}
\text{COMEBACK} = &\ a_0 + a_1\text{SAT} + a_2\text{STUAGE} + a_3\text{MINORITY} + a_4\text{PROFSAL} \\
&+ a_5\text{FACPHD} + a_6\text{E\&G} + a_7\text{JOURNALS} + a_8\text{ONCAMPUS} \\
&+ a_9\text{STUFAC} + a_{10}\text{PTFAC}
\end{aligned} \tag{1}
$$

$$
\begin{aligned}
\text{GETBA5} = &\ b_0 + b_1\text{SAT} + b_2\text{STUAGE} + b_3\text{MINORITY} + b_4\text{PROFSAL} \\
&+ b_5\text{FACPHD} + b_6\text{E\&G} + b_7\text{JOURNALS} + b_8\text{ONCAMPUS} \\
&+ b_9\text{STUFAC} + b_{10}\text{PTFAC}
\end{aligned} \tag{2}
$$

Regression Results. In general, the data fit the two regression models very well, meaning that the two equations were appropriate for the purpose of prediction (that is, for dividing the institutions into productive and underproductive groups). The ten measures of student and institutional characteristics explained 75 percent of student retention (COMEBACK) at doctoral institutions, 50 percent at comprehensive institutions, and 59 percent at liberal arts colleges. These same measures also accounted for 76, 42, and 65 percent of the student graduation rate (GETBA5) at doctoral, comprehensive, and liberal arts institutions, respectively (note that *F*-values for all models were significant at the .001 confidence level).

Productive Versus Underproductive Institutions

Here we present the results of the comparisons between the productive and underproductive institutions and explore potential strategies colleges can employ to improve productivity. In Table 3.1, the productive and underproductive institutions are represented by the HIGH and LOW columns, respectively, with each group further divided according to institutional type and by each of the two student outcome measures.

Table 3.1. Comparisons Between Productive and Underproductive Institutions

VARIABLE	DOCTORAL				COMPREHENSIVE				LIBERAL ARTS			
	COMEBACK		GETBA5		COMEBACK		GETBA5		COMEBACK		GETBA5	
	HIGH	LOW	HIGH	LOW	HIGH	LOW	HIGH	LOW	HIGH	LOW	HIGH	LOW
COMEBACK	84.63	79.36***	88.22	78.51***	80.48	71.10***	79.66	72.48***	86.84	75.39***	87.23	75.91***
GETBA5	58.00	62.92	70.00	55.26***	54.76	49.61*	61.48	45.58***	69.70	59.73***	73.15	56.43***
GOODYEAR	88.0	85.45	90.97	84.32***	85.86	79.95***	86.44	80.44***	90.79	86.74***	91.82	86.47***
SAT	1.1K	1.17K	1.20K	1.15K*	1.05K	1.04K	1.0K	1.04K	1.1K	1.12K	1.1K	1.1K***
STUAGE	21.53	21.61	20.75	21.90***	22.01	22.40	21.91	22.39	20.87	21.35^	20.73	21.39*
MINORITY	14.68	16.89	16.24	16.09	13.69	23.69**	13.54	22.74**	9.18	12.90^	9.77	12.36
PROFSAL	59.84K	60.70K	63.44K	59.20K*	45.93K	47.54K	47.56K	46.65K	42.85K	42.40K	45.76K	40.47K***
FACPHD	0.693	0.695	0.73	0.68	0.54	0.53	0.56	0.53	0.59	0.54^	0.65	0.52**
E&G	16.9K	67.1K	20.4K	61.7K	6.3K	6.30K	6.72K	6.14K	11.1K	9.76K	12.2K	9.26K***
JOURNALS	12.76	16.01	15.3	14.77	8.57	6.68	6.85	7.48	9.54	8.11	9.93	8.0
ONCAMPUS	39.78	45.01	50.33	40.31*	45.50	41.48	48.32	40.79*	73.84	69.12	77.74	67.41***
STUFAC	14.09	14.01	13.35	14.30	17.00	18.98	16.07	19.12*	11.55	12.05	11.05	12.27*
PTFAC	0.31	0.28	0.26	0.31*	0.41	0.41	0.45	0.39	0.37	0.47**	0.36	0.47**
FEDGRANT	36.5K	92.3K	39.4K	86.6K	8.10K	10.3K*	7.0K	10.4K***	6.8K	8.1K	5.9K	8.5K***
T-GRANTS	70.0K	226.0K	85.1K	196.0K	1.57K	1.57K	1.4K	1.6K	24.0K	25.0K	19.2K	27.1K
HS-RANK	64.73	69.56	72.80	65.31	48.11	45.92	49.62	45.48	57.18	51.50^	58.71	50.75*
BOOKS	130.06	139.70	173.10	121.56	62.63	55.54	68.74	54.16*	149.52	131.72	173.96	120.52***
INSTRUCT	0.38	0.38	0.37	0.38	0.39	0.41^	0.37	0.41***	0.31	0.299	0.32	0.30*
RESEARCH	0.15	0.14	0.15	0.15	0.02	0.02^	0.01	0.02*	0.0048	0.0089	0.009	0.006
LIBRARY	0.034	0.035	0.04	0.03	0.04	0.04	0.04	0.04	0.03	0.03	0.04	0.03*
PRI-TIME	1.72	2.25*	2.00	2.10	2.11	1.89	2.12	1.19	2.21	1.99	2.09	2.05
REWARD#	0.36	0.28	0.29	0.33	0.56	0.24**	0.43	0.33	0.19	0.22	0.30	0.18
SAL-INFL#	0.67	0.41^	0.67	0.41^	0.81	0.55**	0.78	0.60^	0.77	0.58*	0.84	0.55**
SAL-COMP#	0.76	0.61	0.81	0.59^	0.81	0.75	0.85	0.74	0.68	0.59	0.76	0.56*
FAC-PROD#	0.56	0.55	0.67	0.45	0.59	0.52	0.65	0.51	0.73	0.55	0.77	0.54*
POL-EVAL#	0.19	0.18	0.05	0.27*	0.19	0.14	0.18	0.15	0.00	0.08*	0.03	0.06
CALC S/F#	0.86	0.68	0.86	0.67	0.91	0.86	0.97	0.84***	0.92	0.91	0.92	0.90
FAC-DECM#	0.66	0.47	0.76	0.41*	0.58	0.53	0.55	0.55	0.65	0.66	0.68	0.65
ADMN-FAC#	0.91	0.85	0.86	0.88	0.83	0.81	0.88	0.80	0.88	0.71*	0.84	0.73
QUAL-DAT#	0.57	0.59	0.57	0.59	0.81	0.61*	0.79	0.64	0.73	0.74	0.82	0.70

Note: ^$p < .10$, *$p < .05$, **$p < .01$, ***$p < .001$ for t-test with group on left; K = thousand. Variables followed by a pound sign (#) are dichotomous variables (1 = yes, 0 = no).

In general, institutions productive on one outcome indicator are also productive on the other student outcome indicator since COMEBACK and GETBA5 are both significantly larger for the HIGH groups regardless of which outcome variable (either COMEBACK or GETBA5) was used for identifying productive and underproductive institutions. A third student outcome variable, GOODYEAR (representing the percentage of freshmen finishing the year in good academic standing), is also significantly larger for the HIGH groups.

Research. Does research compete with or complement teaching? Is there a trade-off between teaching productivity and research productivity? These were two primary questions related to resource allocation and institutional strategy to which we sought answers.

This study produced some striking results. For all three types of institutions, on both student outcome variables, the underproductive institutions generally had *more* federal (FEDGRANT) and total (T-GRANTS) grants and contracts revenue per faculty member than did the productive institutions. And while the differences in total grants and contracts revenue were not statistically significant, federal revenue differences between productive and underproductive institutions were significant at comprehensive and liberal arts colleges. More specifically, FEDGRANT had a significant adverse impact on student retention at comprehensive institutions, and an adverse impact on graduation rates at both comprehensive and liberal arts colleges. The difference between the productive and underproductive institutions was about $2,600 to $3,400 per faculty member. Since both federal and total grant and contract revenue per faculty member are proxies for research emphasis and productivity, it would seem that there might be a trade-off between the teaching and research functions.

Resources. Our next series of questions dealt with institutional resources and how they were allocated. Do expenditures per student make a difference? Is there a resource allocation strategy that improves student outcomes? What happens if an institution does not have enough money or is in financial difficulty? Our findings on these questions were revealing.

One interesting finding was that underproductive liberal arts colleges had significantly lower educational and general expenditures per student (E&G) than did productive colleges. But the real story is what the findings say about the resource allocation strategies of these underproductive institutions. What did they do? First, they spent proportionately less on instruction (INSTRUCT) and library (LIBRARY) functions. Lower spending on instruction translated into lower faculty salaries and a lower proportion of full-time faculty with Ph.D. degrees (PROFSAL and FACPHD, respectively). In addition, faculty compensation did not keep pace with inflation (lower SAL-INFL). Lower library spending translated into fewer books per student (BOOKS) and fewer journals per faculty member (JOURNALS) at these institutions.

These colleges did not pay other, nonfaculty staff well either; the salary scale for all staff was not competitive (lower SAL-COMP). These colleges also had a larger proportion of part-time faculty (larger PTFAC), and they either offered fewer courses or had larger class sizes (both are indicated by larger student-faculty ratios, STUFAC).

Although the differences between the productive and the underproductive groups for the doctoral and comprehensive institutions were not always statistically significant, the same factors and trends related to expenditures, resources, and allocation strategies were generally evident.

Policies and Procedures. The last set of questions addressed by the study centered on institutional policies and procedures. Are certain policies more effective than others for increasing productivity? What, if any, environmental factors characterize productive institutions? What can colleges do to promote student outcomes without spending a lot of money? Again, the results were revealing.

The findings consistently show, for all three types of institutions and for both outcome variables, that productive institutions were *less* likely to have a formal faculty and staff productivity measurement system (higher FAC-PROD) than were underproductive institutions (this difference was statistically significant at liberal arts colleges). A related factor showed similar results. POL-EVAL, representing whether an institution has a mechanism for evaluating policies related to productivity measurement, was significantly *higher* at underproductive institutions, particularly at doctoral and liberal arts institutions. If we take these two variables together, it would seem that formal productivity measurement systems or policies are associated with lower institutional productivity. However, the data do not indicate whether such formal systems generate low productivity in and of themselves or such systems are instituted in response to an already existing condition of low institutional productivity (a classic chicken-and-egg dilemma). If it is true that having a productivity system has an adverse impact on student outcomes, it may be because such a system clashes with academic culture. One possibility is that institutions establishing productivity mechanisms push too hard, creating a hostile working environment and poor relationships between faculty and administrators. Such environments could have a negative effect on faculty attitudes and, consequently, on student outcomes.

Two other variables that seem to work together are FAC-DECM (faculty feel positive about their level of involvement in decision making) and ADMN-FAC (adequate communication channels between administrators and faculty). Productive institutions generally had higher scores on both of these variables than did underproductive institutions. The importance of faculty communication and involvement in decisions is also reflected in the fact that productive colleges were more likely to calculate the student-faculty ratio when there were changes in enrollment (CALC S/F), indicating attention to faculty concerns.

Another finding, consistent with the student development literature, is that on-campus living can be beneficial to student academic progress. Productive institutions had a significantly greater percentage (5 to 10 percentage points more) of their students living on campus (ONCAMPUS) than did underproductive institutions.

The remaining factors examined by this study seemed to affect the three types of institutions differently. For example, doctoral institutions that assessed resource priorities more frequently (PRI-TIME) were also significantly more productive (productive institutions examined priorities, on average, every one to two years compared to every two to three years for underproductive doctoral institutions). On the other hand, comprehensive institutions that had data on the quality of the education provided vis-à-vis their tuition charges did better (QUAL-DAT). Perhaps these institutions pay more attention to students' return on investment. And last, 56 percent of the productive comprehensive institutions rewarded faculty performance by special nonsalary financial rewards (REWARD) as compared to only 24 percent of the underproductive institutions (a statistically significant difference).

Student Characteristics. We expected that student characteristics would play a very important role in institutional productivity, especially as productivity was measured on the basis of student academic outcomes. The importance of student variables is evidenced by the findings. Even though productivity was defined in this study as the difference between actual and expected performance, meaning that student characteristics were figured into the calculation of the expected performance level, underproductive institutions had significantly different student bodies from productive institutions. Underproductive institutions generally had more minority students, older students, fewer students from the top twenty-fifth percentile of their high school class, and students with lower Scholastic Aptitude Test scores (MINORITY, STUAGE, HS-RANK and SAT). It is hard to say why underproductive colleges would have both a more diverse clientele and a greater amount of faculty grant and contract dollars since the data do not indicate whether the grants are for basic research or for applied research and special projects for student services. However, it is clear that these institutions were trying to do too much without adequate resources. The practices of admitting less well prepared students, maintaining diverse clientele, and emphasizing both teaching and research may be more than they can afford. This finding suggests that underproductive institutions could benefit from identifying goals more supportive of student outcomes and by allocating resources more effectively.

Summary

Returning to the questions that opened this chapter, we find that quite a lot has been learned about academic productivity, including how to define, measure, and improve it. We know that any discussion of productivity is not complete unless both outputs *and* inputs are considered together. The results of the two empirical studies presented in this chapter make clear the importance of institutional inputs, whether revenues, student ability and characteristics, or faculty quality. We have also learned about the importance of output mix and the resource allocation principle with regard to measuring an institution's total productivity. Since our measure of institutional effectiveness was based on student educational progress, it was not surprising to find that underproductive institutions received more grants and contracts revenues. There seems to be a trade-off between teaching and research productivity, and institutions need to keep this in mind. And last, we have identified a number of interventions, policies, procedures, and resource allocation strategies that seem to promote institutional productivity as measured by student outcomes.

References

Astin, A. W. " 'Productivity' of Undergraduate Institutions." *Science,* 1962, *136,* 129–135.

Astin, A. W. "Why Not Try Some New Ways of Measuring Quality?" *Educational Record,* 1982, *63* (2), 10–15.

Bowen, H. R. *The Costs of Higher Education: How Much Do Colleges and Universities Spend Per Student and How Much Should They Spend?* San Francisco: Jossey-Bass, 1980.

Clark, B. R., and others. *Students and Colleges: Interaction and Change.* Berkeley: Center for Research and Development in Higher Education, University of California, 1972.

Feldman, K. A., and Newcomb, T. M. *The Impact of College on Students.* San Francisco: Jossey-Bass, 1969.

Garland, K., and Rike, G. E. "Scholarly Productivity of Faculty at ALA-Accredited Programs of Library and Information Science." *Journal of Education for Library and Information Science,* 1987, *28* (2), 87–98.

Gilmore, J. L. *Price and Quality in Higher Education.* Washington, D.C.: Government Printing Office, 1990.

Goodman, H. H. "The Concept of Output in Education." *Educational Forum,* 1979, *44,* 71–82.

Holland, J. L. "Undergraduate Origins of American Scientists." *Science,* 1957, *126,* 433–437.

James, E. "Product Mix and Cost Disaggregation: A Reinterpretation of the Economics of Higher Education." *Journal of Human Resources,* 1978, *13* (2), 157–186.

Kenny, K., Tietjen, L. D., and Witthus, R. W. "Increasing Scholarly Productivity Among Library Faculty: Strategies for a Medium-Sized Library." *Journal of Academic Librarianship,* 1990, *16,* 276–279.

Knapp, R. H., and Goodrich, H. B. *Origins of American Scientists.* Chicago: University of Chicago Press, 1952.

Knapp, R. H., and Greenbaum, J. J. *The Younger American Scholar: His Collegiate Origins.* Chicago: University of Chicago Press, 1953.

Lincoln, Y. S. "The Structure of Promotion and Tenure Decisions in Institutions of Higher Education: A Policy Analysis." *Review of Higher Education,* 1983, 6 (3), 217–231.

Massy, W. F. "Improving Academic Productivity: The Next Frontier?" *Capital Ideas,* 1991, 6 (2), 1–14.

O'Neill, J. *Resource Use in Higher Education: Trends in Output and Inputs, 1930 to 1967.* Berkeley, Calif.: Carnegie Commission on Higher Education, 1971.

Reagan, G. M. "The Concept of Academic Productivity." *Educational Forum,* 1985, 50, 75–85.

Schapiro, M. O. "The Concept of Productivity as Applied to U.S. Higher Education." Paper prepared under contract to the U.S. Department of Education for presentation at the Organization for Economic Cooperation and Development conference on the Concept of Productivity in Institutions of Higher Education, Quebec, Canada, May 25–27, 1987.

Schuttenberg, E. M., Patterson, L. E., and Sutton, R. E. "Self-Perceptions of Education Faculty: Past, Present and Future." *Education,* 1986, 107, 161–172.

Schwebel, M. "Research Productivity of Education Faculty: A Comparative Study." *Educational Studies,* 1982, 13, 224–239.

Skoro, C. L., and Hryvniak, G. "The Productivity of U.S. Higher Education: 1967–1977." *Research in Higher Education,* 1980, 13 (2), 147–187.

Steele, J. M. "Evaluating College Programs Using Measures of Student Achievement and Growth." *Education Evaluation and Policy Analysis,* 1989, 11, 357–375.

To, D.-L. *Estimating the Cost of a Bachelor's Degree: An Institutional Cost Analysis.* Office of Educational Research and Improvement, U.S. Department of Education. Washington, D.C.: Government Printing Office, 1987.

Vardan, S., Smulyan, H., Mookherjee, S., and Mehrotra, K. G. "Factors Encouraging Research Productivity in a Division of General Internal Medicine." *Academic Medicine,* 1990, 65 (12), 772–774.

JEFFREY L. GILMORE *is a research associate in the Office of Educational Research and Improvement, U.S. Department of Education, and has served as an administrator and researcher both on campus and in government.*

DUC-LE TO *is an economist with the Office of Educational Research and Improvement, U.S. Department of Education, specializing in postsecondary education issues.*

As colleges and universities face the need for cost reduction, the noninstructional areas are the first places to look to contain costs and improve productivity.

Assessing Noninstructional Costs and Productivity

Mary Jo Maydew

When colleges and universities begin to face the reality of their need to control costs, their attention first turns almost invariably to the noninstructional areas. This is as it should be. In the past decade, the rate of growth in support costs has been significant, over 60 percent between 1975 and 1985 (Zemsky, 1990, p. 2). Some of this growth can be attributed to forces over which institutions of higher education have limited control, such as the cost of complying with regulations and general price-level increases. However, a significant component of the expansion in noninstructional costs reflects institutional responses to other kinds of pressures such as the demand for increased levels of service, the competitive advantages of additions to and enhancements of programs, and the felt need for more sophisticated administrative operations. Expansion was possible because the revenue was available. However, as the growth in revenues has reached a plateau—and, in some cases, diminished—in recent years, the wisdom of some of these responses must be reconsidered.

Apart from the rapid growth of support costs in recent years, there is a more fundamental reason why it is appropriate for noninstructional costs to be the first target for cost containment. Our purpose as administrators is to support the academic program; in the words of Zemsky and Massy (1991, p. 5A), we are not "the business of the business." That being the case, it is to be expected that institutions will focus first on opportunities for cost containment and productivity improvements among the noninstructional operations.

There is also a third reason, one close to the heart of our efforts as administrators. Unlike our colleagues on the faculty, the tasks of providing cost-effective services and capturing possible efficiencies are regular parts of our ongoing responsibilities. Our presidents and trustees reasonably expect that administrators know how to do these things. The current need for fiscal constraint provides the impetus for more rapid and more comprehensive measures than would otherwise be necessary or, in some instances, possible.

Approaching Improved Productivity

If we agree that our goal is to provide effective, high-quality support services and programs in as cost-efficient a manner as possible—and if we have already made the obvious, ongoing improvements to our operations—how do we deal with the greater level of intensity that we are now experiencing? The answer has two primary aspects: reassessing and agreeing on the institution's priorities and then finding more cost-effective ways to accomplish those priorities. In Bennis's terminology (1991), we need to do the right things and then do those things right. The primary focus of this chapter is on strategies in aid of the latter, but the preeminence of the former warrants mention.

In times of financial constraint, a closely articulated effort in support of the institution's priorities is crucial. Unless those priorities have been identified and agreed on, the most efficient administrative operations may fail to support the institution's goals. A well-designed and functional planning process is vital, as is the institutional readiness for making difficult decisions. Increasingly, colleges and universities will be in the business of determining which programs and services are unique, rather than those that simply add value. Once the agenda is set and understood, the institution can begin working on its accomplishment.

Strategies for Improving Productivity and Reducing Costs

The general approach most likely to improve the cost-effectiveness of support operations examines the outcomes of the planning process, identifies possible opportunities for change, considers the institutional consequences of various options, and looks beyond the current period. This approach accomplishes two important purposes: (1) the change is reasoned rather than merely reactive, ensuring that the institution will not be damaged by responses to short-term exigencies, and (2) the stage is set to take advantage of any opportunity that arises, minimizing the disruption that rapid change inevitably causes. The combination of thoughtful consideration of multiple paths with opportunistic action is very powerful, joining as it does the need for careful design and the ability to take advantage of the moment.

This approach is in contrast to other cost reduction methodologies that are frequently practiced but provide at best only short-term solutions to cost-effectiveness. Across-the-board reductions, in which each operation receives the same target, and their subset, general expense reductions, generally fail for several reasons. First, they deny the reality that operations have different abilities to reduce costs by applying the same measure to everyone. Second, they make institutional choices at the wrong level. Rather than consider at the outset that some programs and services will receive fewer resources, the decisions about where to reduce costs are forced down into the divisions, sometimes into the departments. This fragmentation is unlikely to result in a set of outcomes that represents a coherent whole, much less the best choices for the institution over time. Finally, the vital opportunity to couple reductions in cost with improvements in productivity is lost. The thrust of the exercise is defined as expenditure of less money, with all cost savings equally valued. This presents the real danger that costs that are easily identifiable or are theoretically postponable will be those reduced. I offer the example of deferring funding for physical plant maintenance, a temptation to which many of us have succumbed in the past and that has become a tremendous problem for higher education as a result.

Improving Cost-Effectiveness

Once the institution has gone through the process of articulating and understanding its priorities, progress toward their accomplishment occurs most clearly by reducing the costs associated with low-priority activities. However, an equally important aspect is the examination of even the highest priority programs and services to ensure their cost-effectiveness. These twofold objectives—focusing available resources on higher rather than lower priorities and increasing the productivity of all programs and services—then define the task.

Colleges and universities, like other organizations, tend to grow and adapt in unsystematic ways. An unmet need or an appealing new program is added into the existing organization. Rarely is the new program or service evaluated in the context of the operation as a whole, assigned a relative level of priority, and analyzed to determine how it might most effectively be integrated into a restructured operation while minimizing the additional resources needed. We are all susceptible to the feeling that our operations are highly efficient already, that all the work we do is necessary and important, and that we will need additional resources to perform new tasks.

That approach works reasonably well when additional resources are readily available to meet most of the new needs that regularly occur. I can remember budget processes in the not-too-distant past in which the toughest decisions made concerned which of the myriad new projects to fund with the revenue remaining after all existing programs and services were funded at requested levels. Those days appear to be gone for all of us (and probably never existed for many of us). The new reality suggests that no program or service, however high the priority, is exempt from the need for improvement—in higher quality, lower cost, or both—and that every change is an opportunity for reassessment.

The implications are clear. Resource allocation becomes a continuous process rather an annual budget development exercise, because change happens continuously. To be sure, the annual budget cycle continues to be the area of most intense focus, since it provides a comprehensive and structured process for review of priorities and areas for improving productivity. However, many interim opportunities present themselves: when a position becomes vacant, when new legislation is passed, when problems occur. An institution poised to evaluate and act on changes as they occur will find itself better placed to make maximum use of the budget process and to minimize the disruptive consequences of cost reduction.

A variety of analytical approaches can assist colleges and universities in determining how to improve productivity in noninstructional activities. Some, like Total Quality Management, are discussed elsewhere in this volume. Rather than review the techniques of cost reduction and productivity improvement, I center the discussion here on where to look within the organization and present ideas and examples, some overlapping, of ways to identify possible opportunities for improving cost-effectiveness. Once those opportunities have been identified, the evaluation process can then proceed.

As a matter of convenience, many of the specific examples are taken from work that my colleagues and I are doing at Mount Holyoke College and are meant to be suggestive rather than prescriptive. Each institution is unique and should be so viewed. Individual strategies must be shaped, based on the college and university's culture, history, traditions, and current human and financial resources available.

Consolidation of Organizations. Many colleges and universities continue to have very horizontal organizational structures. Senior managers may have fifteen or more persons with whom a direct reporting relationship exists. Presidents and chief academic officers may have many more direct report staff whose levels of responsibility within the organization vary widely. Inevitable to such structures are difficulties with communications and coordinated effort. Considerable time and energy are necessarily devoted to many people constantly interacting with one another, keeping each other informed, and trying to avoid duplicate or inconsistent efforts.

There are important opportunities to improve program and service delivery and simultaneously to reduce costs through a more streamlined organizational structure. In some cases, it may be as straightforward as combining two departments with similar and overlapping functions into a single overall operation with an integrated focus, for example, development and public relations. In other cases, an existing organization may work better by separating its component parts and combining them with other operations. At Mount Holyoke, we have split the Division of Admissions and Financial Aid into its components, moving admissions into the academic operations and incorporating financial aid into the college's financial functions. There are a variety of individual examples; the key is to find opportunities to combine similar activities without adding layers of management.

Consolidation of Functions. This approach applies the same consolidation principle to a different dimension, that of function rather than structure (Massy, 1991). The benefits are similar. The targets here are similar tasks that are performed in several places. How many people in different departments are involved in publications, or computing, or managing supplies inventories? There are dozens of opportunities in all but the smallest institutions for consolidating similar functions.

However, the benefits in the form of improved service are likely to be more accessible than those in the form of cost savings in all but some areas in very large institutions. It will often be the case that all these similar functions represent small-to-moderate fractions of several employees' jobs. The resulting savings in staff time, while real, can be difficult to capture, since it will require secondary restructurings in those operations. Patience and determination are necessary to guard against the inevitable pressure to fill this saved time with other tasks rather than squeeze the quarter or third of a position out of the department. Patience is particularly important. This sort of downsizing often is best accomplished in combination with the implementation of other productivity improvements or upon the occurrence of a position vacancy in a key area.

Centralization Versus Decentralization. The relative benefits of centralization and decentralization depend on a variety of characteristics, including some that are idiosyncratic to the individual college or university. An institution's culture, the strengths of its management team, and the style of its president will all affect how this basic component of organizational structure is accomplished and the opportunities for modifying the structure. That being said, for most small to medium-sized colleges, and perhaps for some small universities, centralization of structures and functions is likely to both improve the quality and reduce the overall cost of the program or service.

This result is considerably less predictable in large institutions, however. Indeed, for a number of large universities, the trend during the recent past has been toward decentralization as a means of simplifying bureaucracy, assigning responsibility for outcomes, and improving re-

sponsiveness to varying needs. In the universities, the level of centralization is likely to vary widely, perhaps with a bias toward the middle of the
continuum. Even for the very largest institutions, some functions are
usefully centralized, treasury operations, for example, but many others
can be effective within a wide variation of structures. A modest move
toward centralization, or, in some instances, decentralization, on the
margin may well improve cost-effectiveness without damaging the quality of the service provided.

Changing Levels of Service. One of the most difficult areas to
evaluate, because it is so embedded in the existing operations, is the need
to continue the current level of service in any of a number of areas.
Perhaps for that reason, level of service is one of the primary focal points
in many of the resource management techniques that have emerged in
the past two or three decades. Program budgeting, zero-based budgeting,
and Total Quality Management all try to isolate the need for and the cost
of providing services at various levels. Despite the complexity of these
analyses, they offer many opportunities for cost reduction. What is the
utilization of the service? Does it make more sense to stimulate usage or
to diminish availability? Is the service well used but low priority, nice but
not adding value, adding value but not crucial?

One of the difficulties inherent to the task of capturing these kinds of
savings is, in fact, the sheer number of possible places to look. Virtually
every administrative program or service is susceptible to such a review—
from the campus post office to student counseling, from the turnaround
time on accounts-payable checks to how often the dormitories are cleaned.
To be effective in finding ways to reduce costs, such reviews need the
active participation of many people within the institution, particularly
the area managers, who knows the tasks and may best understand the
consequences of change.

There is another way to think about changing levels of service:
regulating the demand through pricing. To address a situation where
access to convenient parking is a scarce resource, an institution might
issue fewer parking permits or increase the cost of parking. Other areas
in which changing the price structure might be more effective than
directly reducing the level of service available include student telephone
access, computer cycle usage, and student access to laser printing.

Uses of Technology. Although higher education as an industry has
been an enthusiastic user of computers, various technological applications continue to help enhance productivity. New communications technologies, such as fax machines, voice mail, and electronic mail, are
efficient and cost-effective supplements, and frequently substitutes, for
written correspondence or telephone conversations. Library automation
can provide electronic access to catalogues at a variety of institutions
and, increasingly, to the collection materials. Computers have long been

used to streamline repetitive tasks and to provide better information and analysis.

Now newer, more accessible technology is reducing the need for administrative support, both secretarial and analytical. As managers, we can perform our own data analysis, develop our own presentation materials, create our own forms, and manage our own correspondence with an efficiency that is increasing rapidly. Cost savings can surely result, but the process may require careful scrutiny of office procedures to identify where the time savings are occurring. As is suggested above, some likely places are the administrative support and analyst staffs. And, again, these savings will almost surely occur in fractions of positions with the attendant difficulty in realizing the cost reduction.

It is important to acknowledge that technology, while reliably an improvement to service, is often anything but a mechanism for cost reduction. In part, this is true because technology improvements may help us to avoid increased costs in the future but by themselves cannot reduce existing costs. Only with a parallel effort to identify productivity improvements, and therefore expected cost savings, can improvements in technology be truly cost-effective (Forum for College Financing, 1991).

Contracting for Services. The make versus buy decision is a fundamental productivity analysis, and one that is being applied to an ever-widening variety of services. The contractual arrangements for campus bookstores, food service operations, and janitorial services are very familiar. But many other possibilities for purchasing services exist that may result in cost savings to colleges and universities: publications, student loan processing, payroll and accounting services, catering, copy services, campus security, construction management, and so on. The key to the make versus buy decision is, of course, the trade-off between cost and quality, as is the institution's own expertise and experience in providing the services under review. A careful and comprehensive analysis is important, but equally important is the willingness to question the status quo, which is often the most difficult part of this effort.

A companion opportunity to enhance productivity is to take maximum advantage of in-house expertise to accomplish efforts that might ordinarily be contracted out. This strategy is particularly available to larger institutions with their greater numbers of employees. However, even smaller colleges, with talented people and careful attention to cost-efficiency, may have opportunities to use existing staff in services from microcomputer repair to trust administration.

Reducing Waste. This approach seeks to remove the inefficiencies in the institution's systems and procedures: errors, duplication, missing links in processes that create confusion, and so forth. Like changes in service levels, waste reduction attempts to change practices that are deeply embedded in the institution and that will require careful and systematic analysis to improve. Nevertheless, the simultaneous improvement of quality and savings in costs that can result from a painstaking effort at waste reduction can be substantial. Identification and correction of these systemic inefficiencies is at the heart of the Total Quality Management discipline.

The opportunities to reduce waste in any organization are myriad; any system or set of procedures is likely to be suboptimal in some ways. The path to success, obviously, is to identify the areas most susceptible to improvement, in quality, cost-efficiency, or both. Predictably, this approach requires knowing the individual institution to determine the most productive areas in which to begin. However, there are some general clues of places to look. How many departments and individuals must be involved to accomplish the process? Is the error rate high? Is the frequency of complaint high? How complicated is the procedure? These and similar diagnostic questions can help to determine the policies for review.

Reviews of systems and procedures with the goals of reducing needless complexity, eliminating errors and the need for rework, and removing steps that do not add value—whether done using Total Quality Management techniques or some other form of analysis—position managers squarely to confront their own bureaucracies. This can be a daunting task, but it is within the details of our administrative operations that much of the growth in cost has occurred. We now need to distill the dozens (or hundreds or thousands) of little inefficiencies that add cost without adding value. These productivity improvements, time-consuming as they can be to tease out of the institutional processes, offer clear value. They lower cost while improving programs and services in contrast to other approaches that often force a choice between level of service and cost.

Particular Problems of Small Institutions

Much of the discussion about administrative cost reduction makes the underlying assumption that there is a considerable infrastructure on which to begin making reductions—layers of management to eliminate, multiple approvals to reduce, Byzantine procedures to simplify. Thus, small institutions face a particular challenge in confronting the need to reduce costs. Across-the-board approaches to cost reduction are not often useful, since in a small operation there are fewer degrees of freedom at the outset. In addition, the variety of programs and services offered in small colleges is likely to be narrower, with fewer optional offerings. This characteristic forces a critical review of the productivity of existing programs and services earlier in the cost reduction process. Finally, a team effort at reduction is even more important at small institutions, since there are correspondingly fewer opportunities to achieve productivity improvements within the sphere of a single manager's operation. As a result, small colleges frequently find it difficult to apply techniques such as those just described to their situations.

It is certainly true that small institutions have fewer layers of management and fewer opportunities for centralization with its companion economies of scale. Nevertheless, there remain a number of opportunities for productivity enhancement available to small colleges, both through creative adaptation of more general techniques and through application of approaches particularly useful in small operations.

Reduction of Specialization. The need to accomplish what in many ways are similar tasks to those performed at a large institution, though in a smaller setting, has frequently meant that one- and two-person offices abound in small colleges. Lacking enough volume of many kinds of work, small institutions often staff operations for the peak effort needed, with the predictable consequence that these specialized employees may not be effectively utilized at other times. Generalization of these positions can frequently result in accomplishment of the same set of tasks with fewer staff and better professional depth in the function. By broadening job responsibilities, increasing cross-training, and building a more encompassing conception of employees' roles, all colleges can replicate the value of consolidation opportunities available to their larger peers.

Opportunities also exist in operations where volume is variable or low but coverage is necessary, such as office receptionists or night telephone operators. These employees frequently have idle time that can be used to assist with peak times in other areas, particularly in handling mailings and other tasks that are straightforward and do not deflect concentration from the primary job function.

Multiple Uses. By finding multiple uses for physical assets, small institutions can simulate economies of scale. The strategy is analogous to reducing specialization in employee functions, but the focus is on the college's plant and equipment. Shared uses may exist within the campus community in areas such as computing, audiovisual equipment, and college vehicles. In addition, there is the important question of how completely the campus is being used—in the evening, in the summer, during breaks—and what other opportunities for its use might exist. Colleges from the largest to the smallest have opportunities for generating additional revenue either from additional programming or from outside use of the campus for summer conferences, community events, and so on. When dealing with use of campus facilities by outside groups, the implications for unrelated business income must be considered, but the opportunities exist to be explored.

Joint Ventures with Other Institutions. Cooperation with other institutions of higher education is another approach that may provide a means of emulating economies of scale. While some institutions such as the Five Colleges Consortium in Massachusetts and the Claremont Colleges in California have a long tradition of intercollegiate cooperation, others have not yet explored such opportunities. At one level, purchasing consortia, insurance captives, and similar joint ventures, which have existed for a number of years, continue to provide cost-effective access to such services. In addition, a number of other opportunities for shared programs and services exist that might be cost-effective in areas as diverse as career counseling, joint health insurance programs, and student loan collections. Finally, new opportunities are developing, either through joint funding or by purchasing service from a larger neighbor, in technically specialized fields such as environmental health and safety, employee assistance programs, and diagnostic testing for students with learning disabilities.

Automation of Manual Processes. Many small colleges continue to have a number of manual systems and processes. However, recent improvements in the availability of sophisticated, but readily usable, software for microcomputers have made it possible for the smallest of institutions to automate their remaining manual processes. While there is certainly some incremental cost in both money and time in making these changes, the opportunity for productivity improvement can be considerable.

The ease of use and flexibility of the new software may also affect the continued cost-effectiveness of contracting decisions. In areas such as forms design and production, in-house publications, manuscript production, and even some accounting functions, campus production may become the lower-cost alternative.

Conclusion

This discussion has centered on a variety of approaches that can assist colleges and universities in reducing the cost of administrative programs and services. While there are many avenues that can productively be pursued in an institution's search for lower administrative costs, the institution must first be ready to make the hard decisions that inevitably come with any cost reduction effort. Our own experiences at Mount Holyoke, and my observations of other institutions' experiences, suggest that cost reduction is most effective when there is a common understanding of the institution's core priorities, a strong and cooperative management team that avoids territoriality and adopts an institutional perspective, and a serious and sustained effort to communicate the need for change, the process, and the desired outcomes to the community.

For those of us who are administrative managers, an important challenge is to accept the reality that administrative retrenchment will be and should be the first order of business in cost reduction. Embrace the necessity. Institutional consolidation of this kind can only happen during periods of financial difficulty. With careful planning and the will to accomplish the task, the institution can emerge from this period of retrenchment better managed, more productive, and fiscally stronger, worthy goals even in good times.

References

Bennis, W. "Leadership for the 1990s." Paper presented at the annual meeting of the National Association of College and University Business Officers, Nashville, Tennessee, July 22, 1991.

Forum for College Financing. "Improving Productivity in Higher Education: Administration and Support Costs." *Capital Ideas,* 1991, 6 (1), 9.

Massy, W. F. "Causes and Cures of Cost Escalation in College and University Administrative and Support Services." In *Proceedings of the National Symposium on Strategic Higher Education Finance and Management Issues.* Washington, D.C.: National Association of College and University Business Officers, 1991.

Zemsky, R. "The Lattice and the Ratchet." *Policy Perspectives,* 1990, 2 (4), 1–8.

Zemsky, R., and Massy, W. F. "The Other Side of the Mountain." *Policy Perspectives,* 1991, 3 (2), 1A–8A.

MARY JO MAYDEW *is treasurer at Mount Holyoke College, South Hadley, Massachusetts, and is a member of the board of directors of the Eastern Association of College and University Business Officers.*

Appropriate indicators for determining academic and administrative costs at a college or university can be useful tools for developing strategies to contain those costs.

Examining Academic and Administrative Productivity Measures

Michael F. Middaugh, David E. Hollowell

Others in this volume have discussed the problem of spiraling costs in American higher education, and the need to develop strategies for containing those costs as a means of keeping higher education affordable and accessible to the general population. Zemsky and Massy (1990) have distilled the factors contributing to the cost pressures in higher education into a useful conceptual framework that they refer to as the "academic ratchet and administrative lattice." In this chapter, we quantify the Zemsky and Massy framework and examine ways in which the University of Delaware has developed analyses to assist in inhibiting and diminishing the forces that drive both the ratchet and the lattice.

The ratchet-and-lattice argument is that, over time, faculty have moved away from their traditional teaching and student advising responsibilities to focus on research and scholarly activity directed at meeting their own needs rather than those of the institution. Functions formerly conducted primarily by academic personnel have been transferred to a burgeoning administrative structure that is characterized by bureaucratic machinations and inefficiencies. Are the academic ratchet and administrative lattice realistic interpretations of the current state of American higher education?

Data developed by the University of Delaware clearly support the ratchet-and-lattice framework. Inflation, as measured by increases in the consumer price index, was 24.8 percent for the period covering fiscal years 1985 through 1991. Over the same period, academic budgets at the University of Delaware grew by 62 percent, administrative budgets by 85 percent, and institutionwide items (fringe benefits, debt service, deferred maintenance costs, and so on) by 63 percent. This budget growth was

New Directions for Institutional Research, no. 75, Fall 1992 © Jossey-Bass Publishers

61

stimulated in large measure by proliferation in the number of employees at the university. Ostensibly, colleges and universities exist in large measure to serve students. Yet, while matriculated student enrollments at the University of Delaware increased by 11.5 percent from fall 1984 to fall 1990, authorized faculty positions increased by 14 percent, graduate student teaching and research assistant positions by 20 percent, salaried staff (nonexempt) positions by 23 percent, and professional (exempt) positions by 48 percent.

The growth in budgets and authorized positions at the university far outstrips two reasonable benchmarks: inflation and growth in student enrollments over a six-year period. Why? If the underlying premise of the academic ratchet is correct, then teaching loads should have declined over the same time frame in order for faculty to pursue their own research and publication interests. In fact, teaching credit hours per full-time equivalent (FTE) faculty did decline 9.1 percent over the past decade at the university, class contact hours per FTE faculty declined 19.5 percent, and student credit hours per FTE faculty declined 16.5 percent. Faculty teach fewer courses, spend less time in the classroom, and have lighter student loads.

At the same time, the administrative lattice interpretation would have us look for growth in nonfaculty positions with responsibility for assuming duties previously handled by faculty. In fact, the number of professional positions *within academic units* grew 52 percent at the university from fiscal year 1985 to fiscal year 1991, and professional positions within administrative units increased 41 percent. These data contrast with a faculty growth rate of 14 percent for the same period. These numbers encompass the addition of new academic programs (for example, a conservatory theater program, a graduate linguistics program, and a hotel and restaurant management program) as well as new administrative functions (for example, a technological outreach office, a glossy alumni magazine, computer networking, and a greatly expanded instructional technology unit). During this time, no academic or administrative programs were eliminated at the university, and Delaware resident tuition and fees increased by 73 percent and those for nonresidents by 80 percent. It is apparent that tuition revenues were being used to underwrite both the decline in average faculty instructional work load and the simultaneous increase in administrative overhead.

Mobilizing the Institution

By fall 1990, it was evident to university planners that significant budgetary pressures endangered the institution's fiscal health. It was evident that if business continued as usual, expenditures would exceed revenues by some $9 million during the 1991 fiscal year. Moreover, the growth in fixed, recurring costs (particularly salaries and fringe benefits associated with the current work force) was such that the institution could expect increasing budget deficits in subsequent years unless preemptive steps were taken.

The university established the Budget Council and charged it with responsibility for institutional budget planning. Chaired by the provost/ vice president for academic affairs, the council is composed of the senior vice president for administration, the university treasurer, and the assistant to the president. The council is augmented by four additional academic advisers, including the associate provost, one dean, and two department chairs, the latter three positions being one-year, rotating appointments. Staff support is provided by the director of institutional research and planning, the director of the budget, and the assistant provost for academic budget planning. The Budget Council meets regularly with faculty, staff, and student constituent groups to apprise them of issues under consideration and to solicit their views.

It is important to emphasize that the process employed by the Budget Council for determining budget reductions and cost containment strategies is designed to be inclusive enough to give the campus community confidence in that process. On the other hand, both the process and the numerical composition of the Budget Council are not so representative as to become bogged down in endless discussion and indecision. The distinction between inclusion and representation is a functionally important one. While input from the full spectrum of campus constituencies is essential, the process must not be so representative that it becomes a "committee of the whole," incapable of making tough decisions.

The Budget Council is faced with the task of recommending targets for cost reductions. The council operates on a basic premise: Discussion of recision and cost containment must never lose sight of the primary reasons for a college or university's existence, namely, teaching and research, activities associated with the classroom and laboratory. Institutional functions that undergird these central mission areas must be protected to the largest extent possible. While aware of that caveat, it is nonetheless evident that most colleges and universities will experience personnel reductions in resolving budgetary difficulties.

Higher costs for more people may be the most powerful mechanism driving the budgetary problems in American higher education today. The sharply escalating cost of employee fringe benefits has played a major role in the financial crises at most postsecondary institutions. Benefit costs escalate on an employee base that is already enlarged as the result of the academic ratchet and administrative lattice forces.

Control of benefit costs is a national challenge that will require more time to achieve than most institutions can afford. Barring major employee concessions in the area of fringe benefits, reduction of the number of employees is the only short-term solution to the problem of reducing the cost of those benefits.

In determining areas for personnel and other budgetary reductions, it is important to use a reasonable set of cost indicators for both academic and administrative units. We have developed such indicators for use at the University of Delaware. These data-based measures are easily replicable at any institution seeking to quantify a basis for cost and productivity analysis. Their development, along with caveats for their use, is detailed in the remainder of this chapter.

Academic Analysis

In analyzing academic productivity, our primary objective was to develop a relationship between teaching activity and the other activities that faculty might perform in lieu of teaching, that is, research and/or public service. More to the point, a means was sought to assess the direct costs of instruction within an academic unit, with an eye toward determining the extent to which nonteaching activity generated revenues to offset those instructional costs.

Table 5.1 contains a sample departmental profile utilizing the instructional productivity indicators that have been established at the University of Delaware. First, it is important to underscore that they are indicators and nothing more. Ratios and trend data are useful for identifying areas for further examination. They are, however, only tools for the process, not ends in themselves.

In examining academic units at the University of Delaware, we considered the following discrete variables in Table 5.1:

FTE Majors. FTE majors, by student level, are calculated by taking the total number of part-time students and dividing that number by three, and then adding the quotient to the total number of full-time students. Long-term or dramatic shifts in FTE majors may well have implications for future resource allocation decisions.

Student Credit Hours. Student credit hours (credit value of courses taught multiplied by students enrolled in the courses) are tallied for lower-division, upper-division, and graduate levels of instruction in both regular courses and supervised study. These data are displayed separately to reflect both *origin of course* and *origin of instructor*. In origin-of-course analysis, the data reflect all student credit hours taught within a given academic department regardless of the "home" department (that is, the department to which salary is budgeted) of the instructor. The extent to which a department is a service department, that is, teaches other than its own majors, is measured through the percentage of origin-of-course student credit hours that is consumed by department majors versus nonmajors. Origin-of-instructor analysis accumulates student credit

Table 5.1. Budget Support Data: Work Load Analysis, 1988-89 Through 1990-91

Department/Unit	Fall 1988	Fall 1989	Fall 1990	Spring 1989	Spring 1990	Spring 1991	Annual Average 1988-89	Annual Average 1989-90	Annual Average 1990-91
FTE majors									
Undergraduate	219	268	297	242	262	308	231	265	303
Graduate	58	74	66	53	68	54	56	71	60
Total	277	342	363	295	330	362	286	336	363
Student credit hours (origin of course)									
Lower division	7,677	7,422	7,122	6,351	5,869	6,153	7,014	6,646	6,638
Upper division	2,488	2,281	2,645	2,451	2,670	3,104	2,470	2,476	2,875
Graduate	420	545	574	415	550	507	418	548	541
Total	10,585	10,248	10,341	9,217	9,089	9,764	9,901	9,669	10,053
Percentage of student credit hours consumed by majors	11.9	15.5	19.2	15.0	18.7	20.5	13.5	17.1	19.9
Percentage of student credit hours consumed by nonmajors	88.1	84.5	80.8	85.0	81.3	79.5	86.5	82.9	80.1

Table 5.1. (continued)

Department/Unit	Fall 1988	Fall 1989	Fall 1990	Spring 1989	Spring 1990	Spring 1991	Annual Average 1988–89	Annual Average 1989–90	Annual Average 1990–91
Student credit hours (origin of instructor)									
Lower division	N/A	N/A	5,532	N/A	N/A	5,383	N/A	N/A	5,457
Upper division	N/A	N/A	2,429	N/A	N/A	3,023	N/A	N/A	2,726
Graduate	N/A	N/A	495	N/A	N/A	514	N/A	N/A	505
Total	N/A	N/A	8,456	N/A	N/A	8,920	N/A	N/A	8,688
FTE students taught (origin of course)									
Lower division	511.8	494.8	474.8	423.4	391.3	410.2	467.6	443.0	442.5
Upper division	165.9	152.1	176.3	163.4	178.0	206.9	164.6	165.0	191.6
Graduate	46.7	60.6	63.8	46.1	61.1	56.3	46.4	60.8	60.1
Total	724.3	707.4	714.9	632.9	630.4	673.5	678.6	668.9	694.2
FTE students taught (origin of instructor)									
Lower division	N/A	N/A	368.8	N/A	N/A	358.8	N/A	N/A	363.8
Upper division	N/A	N/A	161.9	N/A	N/A	201.5	N/A	N/A	181.7
Graduate	N/A	N/A	55.0	N/A	N/A	57.1	N/A	N/A	56.1
Total	N/A	N/A	585.7	N/A	N/A	617.5	N/A	N/A	601.6
Teaching credit hours (origin of course)									
Lower division	109	111	114	99	106	94	104	109	104
Upper division	80	91	114	89	106	103	85	99	109
Graduate	62	100	103	80	99	82	71	100	93
Total	251	302	331	268	311	279	260	307	305

FTE instructional faculty									
Lower division	8.7	9.0	8.7	7.8	8.8	8.3	9.5	9.3	9.1
Upper division	9.0	8.2	7.0	8.6	8.8	7.4	9.5	7.6	6.7
Graduate	7.7	8.3	5.9	6.8	8.3	6.7	8.6	8.3	5.2
Total	25.4	25.5	21.6	23.3	25.9	22.3	27.6	25.2	20.9
FTE faculty on appointment									
Department chair	1.0	1.0	1.0	1.0	1.0	1.0	1.0	1.0	1.0
Bargaining unit faculty	26.5	27.0	26.5	27.0	27.0	28.0	26.0	27.0	25.0
Permanent part-time faculty	0.0	0.5	0.8	0.0	0.5	0.5	0.0	0.5	1.0
Graduate students	10.5	9.5	7.8	10.0	9.0	7.5	11.0	10.0	8.0
Total	38.0	38.0	36.0	38.0	37.5	37.0	38.0	38.5	35.0
Work load ratios (all ratios reflect origin of course data)									
Student credit hours/ FTE instructional faculty	341.8	378.5	457.8	420.0	350.7	412.7	374.9	407.2	506.1
Student credit hours/ FTE faculty on appointment	228.6	254.4	275.0	256.9	242.4	249.1	272.1	266.2	302.4
Teaching credit hours/ FTE instructional faculty	12.0	12.0	12.0	12.0	12.0	12.0	12.0	12.0	12.0
Teaching credit hours/ FTE faculty on appointment	8.0	8.1	7.2	7.3	8.3	7.2	8.7	7.8	7.2
FTE students taught/FTE instructional faculty	23.7	26.2	31.4	29.0	24.3	28.3	25.9	28.1	34.6
FTE students taught/FTE faculty on appointment	15.8	17.6	18.9	17.7	16.8	17.1	18.8	18.4	20.7

Note: FTE = full-time equivalent, N/A = data not available.

hours for all faculty budgeted to a given academic department, regardless of the department in which the course originates. Departments with low origin-of-course student-faculty ratios over time, which show little teaching outside of the department in origin-of-instructor analysis, may have more personnel than can be justified.

FTE Students Taught. With a concept different from FTE majors for a given department, the number of FTE students taught is calculated by converting student credit hours to FTE students as a measure of student demand for teaching. Assuming that the average semester student credit hour load for undergraduates is fifteen, while that for graduate students is nine, these average loads become the respective divisors for total student credit hours as detailed in the preceding paragraph. As with student credit hours, FTE students taught are arrayed by origin of course and by origin of instructor. Low FTE students taught tallies in both origin-of-course and origin-of-instructor analysis over time suggest minimal demand for the teaching resources in a given department.

Teaching Credit Hours. Teaching credit hours are equivalent to the credit value of a course. Thus, a faculty member teaching three three-credit courses has a teaching credit hour load of nine. Teaching credit hours are arrayed in Table 5.1 by origin of course and level of instruction.

FTE Instructional Faculty. Few faculty on appointment actually teach full loads. Some faculty may be exclusively research faculty. Others may teach, but at a reduced load due to research and service considerations (consistent with the academic ratchet concept). Figures for FTE instructional faculty are derived from teaching credit hours. The university's administered contractual load for faculty is twelve teaching credit hours per faculty member per semester. Thus, if the total teaching credit hours accrued to a given department are divided by twelve, the quotient represents the FTE faculty if all faculty did nothing but teach. In those instances, where FTE faculty on appointment exceed FTE instructional faculty by a substantial margin, there is likely a buy out of faculty time for research and/or public service activities. It is therefore reasonable to expect appropriate evidence of externally generated funding for research and service, as well as significant activity in terms of scholarly publication.

FTE Faculty on Appointment. FTE faculty on appointment represents the full-time equivalency for all department chairs, regular full-time faculty, permanent part-time faculty, and graduate student teaching and research assistants whose salaries are budgeted to a given department.

Work Load Ratios. Student credit hours/FTE faculty, teaching credit hours/FTE faculty, and FTE students taught/FTE faculty are straightforward expressions of mathematical relationships between the data elements previously described. Special attention is paid to teaching credit hours/FTE faculty. Assuming that the average university course has a teaching credit value of three, the teaching credit hour/FTE faculty ratio can be used as an expression of the average number of courses taught by faculty on appointment. Coupled with the other work load ratios described above, these measures constitute a valuable barometer for assessing the extent to which the academic ratchet principle is taking hold in a given department within the institution. .

In addition to basic work load ratios, a series of financial ratios have been developed that are also useful in monitoring the ratchet-and-lattice effects within a department. As presented in Table 5.2, these include the following:

External Funding Ratios. Externally sponsored research and service activity in a department may be viewed as a quid pro quo for reduced teaching loads. Data for research and service are extracted from actual expenditures for those functions during a given fiscal year. Each category of external funding is then cast into a ratio expressing sponsored research or sponsored service/FTE faculty. These ratios are particularly useful when examining departments with especially low work load ratios over time. The lower the work load ratio, the greater the expectation for high external support ratios.

Income and Expense Ratios. Instructional cost data have been developed at the university, reflecting direct expenditures for instruction within a given department or unit, as evidenced by relevant account codes within the institutional accounting system. The total instructional cost is then divided by the respective work load measure to arrive at two key ratios: direct instructional cost/student credit hour and direct instructional cost/FTE student taught. If these indicators show significant

Table 5.2. Budget Support Data:
Financial Resources and Ratios, Fiscal Years 1989–1991

Resources and Ratios	FY89	FY90	FY91
Externally sponsored research	$9,756	$8,823	$9,995
Externally sponsored public service	0	0	0
Total external support	$9,756	$8,823	$9,995
External funding/FTE faculty on appointment	$271	$232	$263
Total direct instructional costs	$1,406,776	$1,596,826	$1,614,681
Direct instructional cost/Student credit hour	$71	$83	$80
Direct insructional cost/FTE student taught tuition revenue	$1,036	$1,194	$1,163
Tuition Revenue	$993,216	$1,285,010	$1,691,588
Earned income	$3,118,152	$4,038,652	$4,346,025
Earned income/Total direct instructional costs	2.22	2.53	2.69

Note: FTE = full-time equivalent, FY = fiscal year.

increases over time, the underlying causes merit full investigation. Two additional financial measures are also useful: tuition revenue and earned income. Tuition revenue represents revenues generated through tuition paid by FTE majors in a department. Earned income, on the other hand, represents the per credit hour tuition income associated with the total student credit hour load taught within a given department. While tuition revenue is an interesting measure of financial productivity by a department, more telling is the ratio expressed as earned income/total direct instructional costs. A ratio in excess of 1.0 indicates that the department earns more through tuition revenues associated with teaching activity than it directly expends in the same function. A ratio of less than 1.0 indicates course consumption at a level less than the cost of instruction. This is a valuable measure when used with caution. By nature, some programs (for example, equipment intensive or exclusively graduate) are inherently more expensive than others. To compare the earned income/direct expense ratio for an undergraduate music department or graduate chemical engineering department to a history or English department is not terribly informative, and is likely misleading. Comparisons between and among kindred departments are essential. The ratios are most useful to track performance in a given department over time, or to compare the department with a similar program at a different institution.

The foregoing measures of academic work load and financial performance are tools for determining areas for potential cost containment. The graduate chemical engineering program with modest instructional work load indicators but with substantial external research support may well be making optimal use of existing resources. On the other hand, a social science unit with declining work load measures and no offsetting support measures may actually have more resources than it can justify. Such a disparity would certainly warrant closer scrutiny.

These types of data are used at the University of Delaware to identify and monitor potential areas for budget reduction and cost containment action. These data are widely disseminated and discussed on campus. While no one is eager to assume the role of publicly stating that a particular program should be reduced or eliminated altogether, the broad understanding of the quantitative bases for such decisions makes them easier to accept when such recommendations come forth from the University Budget Council. This is pragmatic evidence of the concept of inclusion in budgetary decision making.

Administrative Analysis

The preceding text describes concrete indicators of productivity and cost. Unfortunately, similar, broadly accepted indicators are not readily available for administrative units. Nonetheless, it is still possible to come to terms with issues of overstaffing and overbudgeting as they relate to administrative offices.

If the administrative lattice concept is predicated on the notion of geometric growth in the number of employees, bureaucratic structures housing those employees, and escalating costs associated with that growth, then an appropriate starting point is a trend analysis over time with respect to the number of authorized positions and the size of basic operating budgets.

Table 5.3 shows such an analysis at the University of Delaware. An important first step in conducting examinations of this sort is to ensure that the structure of the organization in both comparison years is identical. Table 5.3 reflects the growth in authorized positions from fiscal years 1985 to 1991. Before making a comparison between the two fiscal years, administrative reorganizations occurring during the six-year time frame had to be sorted out, and positions shifted so that the 1991 organizational structure is imposed on 1985. For example, if institutional research reports to the senior vice president in 1991, whereas it reported to the Office of the President in 1985, personnel and basic budgets must be housed in the senior vice president's area in both years in order for growth measures to be comparable.

The appropriate adjustments to the respective organizational configurations having been made, the index numbers in Table 5.3 show that the number of authorized professional positions institutionwide grew by 48 percent from fiscal year 1985 to fiscal year 1991; professional positions in academic units increased by 52 percent, while the growth rate for administrative units was 41 percent.

Further analysis revealed that the greatest growth in academic areas occurred in the colleges, the library, and academic computing, while the largest administrative growth occurred in employee relations, administrative computing, government relations (including public and occupational safety), and university advancement. While these data reflect growth in authorized positions, comparable analyses provide insight into growth of basic operating budgets within and among administrative departments. These analyses provide a "first cut" at identifying administrative areas where accelerated growth may have been accompanied by excess personnel and associated budget costs.

In seeking areas for administrative reductions, focal questions that must be addressed are the nature and centrality of a given unit's functions to supporting the overall institutional mission of teaching, research, and service. Can changes in the context of those functions permit streamlining and consolidation to better serve the institution? Continuous monitoring of administrative units within these emphasized areas permits opportunities for evolution of cost containment strategies. For example, the number of authorized positions in computing and network services,

Table 5.3. **Comparison of Authorized Full-Time Positions: 1984–1985, 1989–1990, and 1990–1991**

Positions	1984–1985	1989–1990	Net Gain (Loss) 1985–1990	1990–1991	Net Gain (Loss) 1990–1991	Growth Index 1985–1991
Academic Units						
Faculty	755.8	852.5	96.7	865.3	12.8	1.14
Graduate students	168.7	200.5	31.8	200.5	0.0	1.19
Professionals	306.2	457.1	150.9	465.8	8.7	1.52
Staff	422.8	533.8	111.0	533.5	-0.3	1.26
Total	1,653.5	2,043.9	390.4	2,065.1	21.2	1.25
Administrative units						
Faculty	0	0	0	0	0	—
Graduate students	2.0	4.0	2.0	3.5	-0.5	1.75
Professionals	217.4	306.4	89.0	307.3	0.9	1.41
Staff	578.3	721.3	143.0	697.5	-23.8	1.21
Total	797.7	1,031.7	234.0	1,008.3	-23.4	1.26
Total University						
Faculty	755.8	852.5	96.7	865.3	12.8	1.14
Graduate students	170.7	204.5	33.8	204.0	-0.5	1.20
Professionals	523.6	763.5	239.9	773.1	9.6	1.48
Staff	1,001.1	1,255.1	254.0	1,231.0	-24.1	1.23
Total	2,451.2	3,075.6	624.4	3,073.4	-2.2	1.25

Note: Data are from the basic budget only and reflect July 1 for each year.

the university's administrative computing operation, grew by 40 percent from fiscal year 1985 to fiscal year 1991. Similarly, the growth in academic computing and instructional technology during the same period was 32 percent. Was the growth justified and does current planning provide sufficient resources for existing staffs and budgets?

Functional analysis revealed that growth in administrative computing personnel was associated with a change in vendors and a major upgrade in administrative hardware and software systems. Concurrent moves toward networking personal computers across campus and to providing increasingly decentralized access to management data also required significant human resources for implementation. The growth in academic computing personnel was the product of an institutional commitment to providing and maintaining numerous student computing sites across campus, and to developing and distributing academic software to faculty for use in instruction, and to students.

Within the context of changing fiscal priorities, new functional emphases emerged for both administrative and academic computing. In the administrative area, installation of new hardware and software was completed by 1991. Networking across campus had become virtually the norm. The number of individuals needed to maintain the system is substantially smaller than the number needed to install and implement it. In the academic area, creation of an environment that actively encourages students to purchase their own computers provided an opportunity to reexamine the number of personnel associated with satellite computing sites across campus. Similarly, software developers in instructional technology were moved from the university's basic operating budget to self-supporting funds generated from sales revenues. Finally, with administrative and academic computing housed on the same mainframe, the decision was made to consolidate staff and to eliminate duplicative organizational hierarchies. The net savings from this functional analysis have been a reduction in excess of thirty authorized positions associated with computing over the past three years.

The emphasis on state-of-the-art administrative computing permits other economies. Where personnel in the Registrar's Office were essential to generating transcripts, auditing degree requirements, producing grade rosters, and similar clerical activities, automated access to an interactive, on-line student record system reduces the demand for those personnel and affords opportunities for consolidation. Enhanced automated reporting systems associated with decentralized data bases similarly reduce the number of individuals needed for generation of paper reports in the full spectrum of administrative areas. The functional analyses that enabled streamlining of computing and associated administrative functions are equally applicable to noninstructional areas of operation.

While the university's top priority in administrative cost containment is a functional analysis of organizational units to ensure that both personnel and operational budgets are in line with institutional objectives, data in addition to the functional analysis also prove useful in monitoring productivity and efficiency.

Staffing ratios between and among personnel classes, that is, faculty, professionals, and salaried staff, are instructive. One would expect different ratios of support staff to faculty in chemical engineering compared to history, the former having significant paperwork associated with sponsored research activity in addition to the teaching and service functions. Similarly, one would look for larger ratios of support staff to professionals in transaction-intensive operations such as accounting and records offices.

While intramural comparisons are useful, data-sharing consortia such as the Public University Information Exchange and the Higher Education Data Sharing Consortium make uniform and consistent interinstitutional comparisons possible. Comparison of instructional work loads between a history and a political science department at the same institution is a legitimate analysis; that analysis is significantly strengthened when those two departments are compared with the same departments at a comparable peer institution. The data-sharing consortia routinely conduct studies and gather data that enable interinstitutional comparisons of both academic and administrative work loads, staffing and funding patterns, and other variables across the universe of institutions participating in the consortia. Representatives from these consortia routinely organize special interest meetings at the annual Association for Institutional Researchers Forum.

Conclusion

Some final thoughts on cost containment analysis in the academic and administrative arenas are as follows: (1) The focus should be on specific programmatic cuts and restructuring of functions in both academic and administrative operations. Effective planners will avoid the easy way out, which calls for across-the-board budget reductions. (2) Consider new and innovative ways to do things. Step back from the traditional organizational structure and look at process. Can functions be combined? Can steps in the process be eliminated? (How many signatures on an authorization are *really* essential?) Determine whether paperflow can be reduced as well as the number of people handling the paper. Ask the question, "What value is added by each person and step in the process?" Consider new paradigms such as Total Quality Management (see Sherr and Teeter, 1991; Heverly and Cornesky, this volume). Be creative. It is possible to reduce costs and improve services when serious people put their minds to it. (3) Carefully examine how technology can be used to support some of the considerations described in the prior section of this chapter. For too long, return on investment in technology has not been a major emphasis. The time has arrived for technology to be put to work to streamline administrative and support functions. (4) Consider privatization (contracting out to external agencies) of supporting services such as dining, bookstore, and custodial and maintenance operations. This may not be advantageous to every institution, but it has proved an extremely viable strategy at many and is worthy of exploration. (5) Do not overlook the opportunity to make organizational and staffing changes that would not otherwise be possible without extreme budgetary pressures. There can be some silver linings in the storm clouds. (6) When personnel reductions are inevitable, give the affected employees as much notice as possible, getting notifications out in the shortest possible time frame. Arrival at the point where it can be announced that layoffs are over for the current year substantially reduces anxiety and increases morale among remaining personnel.

This chapter has described one institution's approach to productivity analysis and cost containment strategy. The framework developed in this chapter is practical, and any college or university can use it. The analytical tools described here are not blueprints for effective cost containment policies. They are simply guideposts that, when viewed within a specific institutional context, suggest areas where program personnel and associated costs might be reduced. The collective wisdom of an institution's leaders is the indispensable ingredient for ensuring the success of productivity and cost analyses.

References

Sherr, L. A., and Teeter, D. J. (eds.). *Total Quality Management in Higher Education.* New Directions for Institutional Research, no. 71. San Francisco: Jossey-Bass, 1991.

Zemsky, R., and Massy, W. E. "Cost Containment: Committing to a New Economic Reality." *Change*, 1990, 22 (6), 16–22.

MICHAEL F. MIDDAUGH *is director of institutional research and planning at the University of Delaware, Newark, and is past president of the North East Association for Institutional Research.*

DAVID E. HOLLOWELL *is senior vice president for administration at the University of Delaware and was national chair of SCUP 27, the 1992 meeting of the Society for College and University Planning.*

The University of Michigan's initiatives for improvement in the 1990s build on its strengthening efforts of the 1980s. The changes made in both decades are intended to ensure that the university continues its tradition of academic excellence and leadership as it moves into the twenty-first century.

Renewal in the 1990s: The University of Michigan Initiatives

Marilyn G. Knepp

The University of Michigan, a public research university, is considered a leader among America's universities. From our earliest days, we have been known as "the mother of state institutions" (Slosson, 1921, p. 169).

Like most colleges and universities, during the 1980s we weathered economic bad times and experienced times of relative prosperity. Our ability to respond to changing conditions and to maintain financial stability during that time was because of continual efforts to contain costs, to reallocate, and to enhance revenues. Much of what we have done has served as a model for other colleges and universities in their efforts to deal with financial stringencies.

Now we face the decade of the 1990s, which we project to be a time of even greater fiscal constraint than the 1980s. How do we come up with new solutions to recurring problems? Are new solutions necessary? What did we learn from the 1980s?

What follows is a case study of how the University of Michigan is attempting to answer these questions today. I begin with a basic description of the university, its historical context, and its analysis of events of the 1980s. The main focus of this chapter is on recent efforts to prepare for meeting the problems of the 1990s. While it is often difficult to generalize from any one case study, it is hoped, nonetheless, that much of what we have done and learned in the process is useful to other colleges and universities as they deal with their own particular situations.

NEW DIRECTIONS FOR INSTITUTIONAL RESEARCH, no. 75, Fall 1992   © Jossey-Bass Publishers

The University of Michigan

The University of Michigan is a large and complex institution. As I shall demonstrate here, size and complexity are both assets and obstacles when dealing with issues of cost containment and improved productivity. To set the stage for this discussion, some background information may be useful. Our enrollment is stable at about 36,500, one-third of whom are graduate or first-professional students. There are 3,200 instructional faculty and about 16,500 other regular employees, 7,000 of whom are in our hospitals. Our annual all-funds budget is about $1.8 billion. The general operating fund accounts for $606 million, with 42 percent of the revenues in the general fund derived from state appropriations, 48 percent from student tuition and fees, and 8 percent from indirect cost recoveries from sponsored research.

The public universities' relationship with the state in Michigan is different from those that exist in most other states. The University of Michigan is guaranteed institutional autonomy by the state constitution. We receive an annual lump sum appropriation of about $257 million in the general fund with minimal restrictions on its use. We determine all of our own policies and practices, from setting tuition rates and keeping all revenues, to what programs we offer and whom we admit. This constitutional autonomy is meant to allow the public universities in the state to operate without the interference of political meddling; and although politics play a role in the determination of appropriations levels, on the whole the university operates independently of state government. It is this autonomy that has allowed the university, especially in times of adversity, to be flexible in responding to changing circumstances in ways that most benefit the institution.

The value of autonomy as a strategic asset was demonstrated vividly in the early 1980s when the state of Michigan experienced a significant recession, which was more extreme and of longer duration than that experienced nationally. The University of Michigan received cutbacks in state appropriations during those years, but because of our ability to compensate for decreases in one general fund revenue stream with increases in others, we did not have any years of actual overall budget cuts. In fact, our general fund budget grew at an average rate that was 2.5 percent higher than inflation as measured by the Higher Education Price Index.

Beginning in the late 1970s, reallocation became an annual occurrence at the university. It has played a critical role, especially during the lean years, in providing flexibility for maintaining financial stability and funding new priorities. The university reallocated, on average, 1.3 percent of the general fund budget every year for a total of $62 million in real terms over the decade. Real growth in research volume of 43 percent also provided new revenue as well as support for the reallocation process.

That growth and reallocation funded many new, exciting ventures on campus—new intellectual directions, explosions of information technology, commitments to recruitment and retention of minority and women faculty and minority students, financial aid growth that outpaced tuition rate increases, and salary programs and benefit compensation exceeding the consumer price index, thus resulting in real increases in average faculty salaries.

Despite all of these positive outcomes of growth and reallocation, when we look back on the decade, the prevailing perception on campus is that they were not very good years. There were constant worries about the state situation; we expended a great deal of effort in planning designed to counteract the deficiencies in state funding. That led to a constant squeeze on our students from spiraling tuition rates and on all university units from the requirements for substantial annual reallocation.

The 1980s were filled with change. We had strong leaders willing to make difficult decisions, we had effective planning programs, and we implemented many changes in our budgeting procedures and policies. However, it took substantial effort to accomplish what we did, and it is important to remember that we enter the 1990s fatigued from the efforts required to get through the 1980s.

Understanding the Past While Setting the Stage for the Future

Many recent publications have helped define the problems facing higher education as we enter the last decade of this century. We have benefited particularly from the works of the Pew Higher Education Research Program and other works by Robert Zemsky and William F. Massy (for example, Zemsky, 1990; Zemsky and Massy, 1991), which both frame the issues and offer solutions. But even those works that only define the problem or, in some cases, fuel the criticism have contributed to our ability to understand our unique situation.

As a result of these external views and our own internal concerns, we recently conducted three major analyses intended to provide a factual basis for the discussion of the University of Michigan's position, problems, and remedies. Each of the three data analyses was conducted by institutional research and budget office staff members at the request of the provost. These data analyses, which are described below, and other corollary data were used by the members of the University Task Force on the Costs of Higher Education. Their deliberations led to a major report to the university community, which is also described here. It contained a series of recommendations that formed the blueprint for new approaches to solving current and expected future problems.

Costs Analysis. The first analysis was a major review of University of

Michigan costs during the 1980s, which the provost requested prior to announcing his intention to form the Task Force on the Costs of Higher Education. He labeled this a preliminary study and presented the results himself at a regents' meeting just after naming the members of the task force. This study was intended to be the major data source for the work of the task force and was guided by the most prevalent criticisms aimed at higher education in general.

The analysis focused on the general fund and the changes in expenditures over the decade relative to inflation. From this analysis, the university learned that contrary to popular perceptions, faculty productivity measured by student credit hour production and research output had not decreased; faculty salaries had shown modest real growth over the decade, enough to recover from the losses incurred in the 1970s; total expenditures on faculty and staff compensation (salaries and benefits combined) were not the primary cost drivers of the 1980s, rather, space costs, information technology, and student financial aid were.

By examining the inverse relationship between tuition and state appropriations, this analysis also responded to the often-asked question, "Why is tuition rising faster than inflation?" First, it explained inflation and then examined the relationships of tuition rates, net tuition revenues (gross tuition revenue increases, student financial aid increases), state appropriations, and overall budget growth.

Staffing Analysis. The second major analysis looked at trends in staffing patterns. This was partly fueled by articles such as Grassmuck's (1990), which featured the University of Michigan and cited staff growth as a major contributing factor to rising costs at universities. The article implied that such growth was evidence of bloat and sloth and echoed continuing charges from our own faculty of excessive growth in administration.

The staffing analysis sought to increase understanding about the amount and sources of growth that had occurred by looking at funding source, job families, and organizational placement. Much of the growth in staff at the university was funded by other than general funds. Our research volume had grown 132 percent over the decade, and there were many more staff appointed on funded research projects by the end of the decade than at the beginning. We had replaced our old main hospital with a new, larger facility and several corollary facilities were renovated or replaced. Staffing at the hospitals, supported on the auxiliary fund by hospital-generated revenues, accounted for a major portion of the staff growth cited in Grassmuck (1990).

Although our analysis clearly countered some of the charges that had precipitated it, it also provided evidence that more attention to our staffing patterns and numbers was in order. There had been growth in staff on the general fund, primarily small increases in any one unit, but growth, nevertheless, in almost every unit. Further, administrative staff growth in the academic units was somewhat greater than central administrative staff growth, although the widely held perception was that the schools and colleges were lean and central administration was not.

Revenue Analysis. The third analysis was a revenue crystal ball that focused on the revenue streams of the general fund. We presented the history of each revenue source over the past decade, explaining how increases had been achieved, and then projected each revenue stream to 1995 based on a set of realistic assumptions. This revenue analysis has been an important tool in promoting recognition of the constrained circumstances that face us in the years ahead.

The revenue analysis convinced us that, regardless of the perception, the 1980s really were "the good old days," the likes of which we were not going to see again in this century. The University of Michigan had enjoyed a period of relative prosperity even during times of state adversity. We had accomplished that by examining each revenue stream and exploiting its potential to the fullest. That meant, however, that all the apparent revenue increase mechanisms already had been employed, and our projections reflected that fact. Prior to this analysis, the provost would tell the deans that tough times were ahead and the deans would be skeptical because the provost "always says that." This analysis was a graphic representation of the gaps between even optimistic assumptions of revenue growth and what would be needed to achieve the university's aspirations.

Impact of the Three Analyses. The data used in the analyses of costs, staffing, and revenue were fairly standard items, although, as is often true here and elsewhere, such data are not necessarily easily obtained or used. The impact that the analyses had was strengthened by the timeliness of the presentations and the particular combinations of topics. We had not previously looked at the questions in precisely these ways, nor had there been such compelling reasons to pay attention to the results.

Each of these analyses has proved useful in many different forums. The revenue analysis has been updated and revised many times to serve particular purposes. The costs and the staffing analyses are scheduled for periodic update and distribution as long as they are still providing useful information to the university community.

Task Force on Costs of Higher Education

The primary purpose of the costs analysis was to serve as the factual basis for the work of the Task Force on the Costs of Higher Education, a group announced by the president in January 1989 and appointed by the provost in March of that year. The task force met regularly for a year. The costs analysis and the revenue analysis combined to their understanding of the Michigan situation, as did an earlier version of the staffing analysis and other analyses commissioned by the task force.

The task force was chaired by Gilbert R. Whitaker, Jr., then dean of the business school, now provost at Michigan. The task force was charged to investigate the costs of higher education at the University of Michigan, to place those costs within state and national contexts, and to develop new and imaginative ways to curtail cost increases while maintaining or enhancing the quality of our programs.

The task force report, *Enhancing Quality in an Era of Resource Constraints,* was released in June 1990. The task force viewed the report as the first step in a longer process. It was not a perfect report with a well-formulated plan but rather a conceptual "think piece" for change. The intent was to lay issues and recommendations before the university community and begin a process of change. The task force deliberately chose not to make specific recommendations about budget priorities or reductions but tried instead to provide a framework for change that, if followed, would lead to significant improvements in the university's ability to achieve its objectives in the coming years. The report contained many recommendations, both specific and general, which can be grouped into three categories: (1) cultural change, (2) a quality approach, and (3) budgeting and planning systems.

Cultural Change. The task force said that the university needed to make a fundamental change in the culture of the organization. The key component of this change should be a simultaneous focus on quality improvement and cost containment. Elements within that framework included the following:

More Focus. We need to be able to ascertain and state the institution's mission, vision, and values and to base decisions on them. This university, like all others, cannot continue to try to do everything, to cover every subspecialty, nor to accede to all demands for new services or new activities.

Less Control and Oversight, More Accountability. Many of our current policies are designed to elicit multiple layers of approval for every action prior to its occurrence, policies that contribute to increased bureaucracy and its attendant frustrations and costs. Units and managers should be held accountable for their decisions and actions but not hampered in the execution of them.

Move Decision Making Down in the Organization. Decisions should be made at the lowest level possible, and local decision makers should understand their rights and responsibilities in doing so.

More Risk Taking, Less Consensus Management. The preferred style of university decision making is consensual, both when appropriate and when not.

Realize the Full Potential of All People in the Organization. Universities believe that people are their greatest, enduring resource yet often act in ways contrary to that belief. Changes in the culture so that policies and actions contribute to the realization of this goal will contribute immensely to the continuing success of the institution.

A Quality Approach. An understanding of the theory of quality improvement is an essential component of strategic planning, and implementation of the principles will lead to reduced costs while enhancing the quality of the institution (see Heverly and Cornesky, this volume). Further, it is as important to apply these principles to the academic enterprise as it is to the management of the university.

The report contained a discussion of the theory and history of quality, along with the ideas of Total Quality Management, and urged the university to adopt such an approach, both academically and administratively. The approach should include elements such as the following:

Customer Orientation. The legitimate needs of the customer should be a factor in determining the requirements of any product or service. While acknowledging the difficulties that the word *customer* presents within an academic environment, the task force endorsed the concept of customer involvement and the importance of precisely defining customers and identifying their legitimate needs.

Take Work Out of the System. One of the primary goals in adopting this approach is to make the university simpler and less bureaucratic, to take work out of the system in order to free human resources to concentrate on the primary goals and mission of the university.

Statement of Mission. Not only should the university state its mission clearly so that decisions can be made congruent with it, so too should the units of the university, whether academic or administrative, state their missions; and their activity decisions should then flow from those missions.

Innovation by Substitution. Akin to Zemsky and Massy's "growth by substitution," for every new activity that we choose to pursue, some other existing activity must be discontinued in order to free the resources for the new activity.

Have Continual Improvement as a Goal. It is certainly the belief of the University of Michigan that we have always aspired to continual improvement of the institution. The report urges the community to explicitly state improvement as a formal ongoing goal so that it becomes a widely shared and understood ideal.

Budgeting and Planning Systems. The last major set of task force recommendations pertained to the budgeting and planning activities of the university. In order to understand these recommendations, it is important to establish the context for our current budgetary activities. Just as the university enjoys autonomy from the state, so too our separate budgetary units enjoy autonomy from the central administration.

The university receives an annual appropriation from the state, sets tuition rates, and collects tuition revenue. The provost, who is the chief budget officer, makes decisions about budget allocations, but once a dean or director receives that budget, he or she is free to make whatever decisions are best for that particular unit. In a sense, each unit receives an annual lump sum allocation and unit budget officials do with it as they will. This makes them responsible for expenditure control but lets them operate independently of revenue generation considerations.

During the 1980s, we changed a number of our budgetary practices under a program known as management incentives. This program was one response to the fiscal crisis of the early 1980s and was intended to introduce the element of unit expenditure responsibility in areas where it previously did not exist.

Our handling of staff benefit expenses is a good example of one of the management incentives. Prior to the implementation of management incentives, the university budgeted staff benefits in a central pool account. A unit budget was responsible for paying an employee's salary, but the staff benefits were funded from the central account. If a unit hired two half-time people to do a job that was formerly done by one full-time person, the unit budget expenditure for salary remained constant. However, the central staff benefits pool account would then be charged for full benefits for two people instead of one, an expensive increase of which the unit manager could be oblivious.

It is our belief that the employing unit should bear the costs of decisions such as these and either pay the costs associated with them or enjoy the use of any savings generated by them. To implement that practice, the central benefits pool was distributed to the units based on the prior patterns of use, and now the separate budgetary units pay both salaries and benefits from their own accounts. In the example cited above, a unit now would realize that replacing a full-time person with two half-time people costs about 15 percent more and would pay accordingly. Similarly, if a unit replaces two half-time people with one full time, then the savings generated would be available for use in other ways.

The task force recommended that we, once again, examine our budgeting practices to ensure that proper incentives exist to encourage good management and decisions and that all disincentives for such are removed from the system.

Recognize Full Costs. There are still some areas where the costs of decisions are not borne fully by the unit making those decisions. At the current time, for example, our budgeting practices do not include any recognition of the costs of the general fund space used by a unit. Utilities, custodial services, maintenance, and security are significant cost drivers within the university, as are capital expense and ongoing expenditures for space increases. If we could implement a change to our budgeting system so that space was no longer a free good, then it might result in more prudent and creative use of existing space as well as preclude the need for new buildings, all of which would hold down costs.

Tie Unit Budgets to Activities in a Direct Way. Units control the expenditure side of their budgets in our current system. However, a unit's budget allocation, the revenue side, has no direct tie to its activities or changes in them. For instance, a unit's enrollment might increase so that the university collects more tuition revenue from students in the unit. But increases in enrollment do not lead to any direct increment in the unit's budget. This situation causes two main problems. The first, of course, is that increases in activities almost certainly impose new costs on the unit. Yet, the increased revenues generated by the activity accrue to the general fund for discretionary allocation by the provost, while the unit is responsible for funding the resources needed to mount the venture. The second drawback is that there are no incentives to find new means to increase overall university revenues because the effects of such changes are not felt locally. In fact, there is an incentive to decrease activities regardless of the overall effect on the university's revenues because the unit is affected only by the expenditure side of an activity, not by its revenue production.

The best management occurs in a situation where the manager is responsible for both the revenue and expenditure sides of the budget. We have an enormously talented and entrepreneurial set of deans who have found creative means to manage within our current system. Once they are responsible for both sides of the ledger sheet, we expect the same spirit to result in a management of revenues with concurrently wise expenditure management.

These budgeting principles are in place at many private institutions, and it is our challenge to adapt them successfully at the University of Michigan. Colleagues from many other universities have graciously shared materials, ideas, and expertise with us as we have attempted to adapt these principles. (Whalen [1991] is a good source for the reader who wants to learn more about this subject.)

Expand the Time Frame of Budgeting and Planning. Our system currently follows an annual cycle. Budgets for one fiscal year are set just at the beginning of that fiscal year, and the following year's allocation is not even hinted until very close to the start of that following year. It is not surprising that our effective planning follows the same annual cycle. Although we have bouts of longer-range planning, they are far more tentative and always subject to revision by the annual budgeting process. The task force recommended that the provost begin formulating and following multiyear plans with some of the academic units to encourage longer-range planning and facilitate implementation of plans.

Budget Revenues First. As is true at most institutions, our budget is formulated in an iterative process where we first decide on an overall expenditure level that is adjusted after annual state appropriations are known or finalized, and where tuition rate increases are based on both expenditure desires and tolerable levels of change. The task force suggested that the university budget revenues first, primarily tuition, and then decide on allocations to meet priority needs, rather than decide on needed levels of expenditures and then set tuition rates accordingly. This move would put us on a "revenue diet," as our provost calls it, which would force us to exercise restraint and presumably tighten decision making. This diet would lead to a better university, but it requires discipline.

Continuing Improvement and Renewal

We believe that the 1990s will be years of change for us, as significant as that experienced in the 1980s. Our institutional goal is to meet and shape the challenges that lie ahead, with the overall excellence of the university as the primary objective. Anticipation of hard times to come has not lessened our expectations for the university, but we recognize that those expectations will be harder to realize. The recommendations of the task force provided the university with a new conceptual framework for identifying solutions to the problems of the 1990s.

Although these recommendations are presented here in three broad categories, they are in fact interdependent and related. The University of Michigan has made progress in many areas mentioned in the report, but the process of change is ongoing and lengthy. The provost is finding that it is easier to be chair of a task force that recommends fundamental change than it is to be the provost who attempts to implement that change. Nevertheless, the leaders of the university are not daunted by the size of the task that faces them.

As change is implemented, it will be important to learn from our successes and failures. Just as we have benefited from the experiences of other colleges and universities, so too we hope that what we learn as we meet the challenges of the 1990s will prove useful to others.

References

Grassmuck, K. "Big Increases in Academic-Support Staffs Prompt Growing Concerns on Campuses." *Chronicle of Higher Education,* Mar. 28, 1990, pp. A1, A32–33.

Massy, W. F., and Zemsky, R. (eds.). *The Dynamics of Academic Productivity.* (J. R. Mingle, comp.) Denver, Colo.: State Higher Education Executive Officers, 1990.

Slosson, E. E. *The American Spirit in Education: A Chronicle of Great Teachers.* New Haven, Conn.: Yale University Press, 1921.

Whalen, E. L. *Responsibility Center Budgeting: An Approach to De-Centralized Management for Institutions of Higher Education.* Bloomington: Indiana University Press, 1991.

Zemsky, R. "The Lattice and the Ratchet." *Policy Perspectives,* 1990, 2 (4), 1–8.

Zemsky, R., and Massy, W. F. "The Other Side of the Mountain." *Policy Perspectives,* 1991, 3 (2), 1A–8A.

MARILYN G. KNEPP is director of the Office of Academic Planning and Analysis at the University of Michigan, Ann Arbor. She served on the University of Michigan Task Force on the Costs of Higher Education.

Lessons from the past, research and analysis, and a focused sense of mission provide direction in a college's quest for academic excellence in an unfavorable financial climate.

Repositioning for the Future: Franklin and Marshall College

Richard B. Hoffman

There is an old curse, "May you live in interesting times." Many of us in higher education are beginning to feel that, for some inexplicable reason, we have become victims of this curse. Although the times are interesting, we have probably made them more interesting than they need be. For the last twenty years or so, senior administrators at independent colleges have been in a constant struggle, first to survive deficits, then to persevere through a long period of high, even double-digit, inflation, and finally to repair the damage wrought during those troubling years. During those years, our focus was principally on an expanding expenditure base, when program revenues were pressed to the limit.

Now we suddenly find ourselves face-to-face with what Zemsky and Massy (1991) have called a "revenue diet," which, even if it is undeserved and ill-timed, appears inescapable. This revenue diet—a set of severe constraints on our capacity to generate annual increases in revenue—is forcing most colleges to give serious attention to material reductions in expenditures. For some colleges, even in the short term, the revenue diet raises questions of survival; for others, such as Franklin and Marshall college, the primary consequence is the reallocation of resources. Most colleges will probably choose a word such as *reposition,* rather than *retrenchment,* to describe their actions, but there is a subtle difference between the two. The latter infers a reduction, rather than a reallocation, in expenditure authorizations.

Although retrenchment in higher education is not a new phenomenon, this most recent period of financial stress appears to be exceptionally severe. For example, Allan Ostar, recently retired president of the American Association of State Colleges and Universities, describes this

NEW DIRECTIONS FOR INSTITUTIONAL RESEARCH, no. 75, Fall 1992 © Jossey-Bass Publishers

economic downturn in higher education as the worst he has seen in his twenty-six years with the association (Cage, 1991). Zemsky and Massy (1990) are also convinced that the climate has changed, and has been changing, in a fundamental fashion, and they foresee a relatively lean future for higher education.

In retrospect, the past decade does not seem so bad after all. During the ten years ending in 1990, the median increase in total current revenues among Pennsylvania's independent colleges and universities was approximately 11 percent annually. After adjusting for inflation, which increased at an annual rate of 4.7 percent, the residual represented a real annual growth rate in excess of 6 percent. The problem, as Zemsky occasionally and insistently reminds us, is that we did not appear to notice—our attention and planning were constantly focused on the many new, important program initiatives that we were hoping to undertake, and we were seeking even greater funding, both for operating and capital purposes.

Among the many factors that affected and still influence revenue and expenditure patterns among the independent institutions are increased competition for students, accompanied by pressure to constrain tuition costs; increased competition for gifts and grants; real decreases in government support; a high dependence on personnel costs; the impact of government regulations; and the continuing need to invest in academic, faculty enrichment, and student support programs.

Although a "no-frills" college has a certain appeal to some, it has none among knowledgeable parents or their children, nor among those whose continued employment depends on filling a freshman class. Those of us who have opportunities to view other colleges closely observe that there is little outright waste. For the most part, programs supported by the operating budget are valuable to students and/or the community. The challenge to reallocate resources, therefore, is no easy task, and little guidance has been offered to those of us who are inevitably charged with the responsibility.

Lessons from the Past

Among the senior planners and administrators of today are a few who experienced the early 1970s, a time described by Cheit (1971) as the "new depression in higher education." This period was characterized by deficits and financial crises leading to extensive retrenchment—yes, retrenchment—even at many of the most prestigious colleges and universities. Some less fortunate institutions closed completely, merged with other colleges, or changed so greatly that they are no longer recognizable as the institutions they once were.

For many institutions, the management response during this time was shared austerity. A number of colleges, including Franklin and Marshall, placed considerable power in faculty-dominated committees charged with advising presidents and trustees, and, for all practical purposes, their advice was followed. At other colleges, senior administrators were left to determine which reductions were to be made. Retrenchment measures were often implemented in an atmosphere of shock and near panic, with little hope for a meaningful recovery.

Typically, employee numbers were reduced—faculty tenure track appointments were not renewed, staff and administrative positions were eliminated—and subsequent salary increases were low or nonexistent, program support was slashed, and funding for maintenance was drastically reduced. At Franklin and Marshall, for example, the faculty size was decreased from 154 positions in 1970 to 115 by 1972, and salary increases for fiscal years beginning in 1971 and 1972 were 1.2 percent and 9 percent, respectively. Funds for travel, equipment, and supplies were greatly reduced; contingency, discretionary, and innovation funds were cut or eliminated.

Most colleges, as we now know, experienced a slow recovery, and some colleges flourished, making significant gains toward their Platonic ideals of excellence. However, our experiences at Franklin and Marshall during those early years of recovery led us to several major conclusions that we believe are important to the task now before us:

1. For nearly all of us in higher education, retrenchment was absolutely essential, and those institutions that moved early and decisively were rewarded greatly in the next decade.

2. The freezing of faculty salaries, even when recommended by faculty committees, was and remains a bad idea—talented, productive people must be compensated fairly. Expectations regarding compensation adjustments after the crisis had passed were not clarified in advance and varied wildly. The financial damage resulting from this compensation policy required a decade to repair, and the publicity surrounding the general decline in faculty compensation was surely a factor in discouraging students from considering teaching as a career.

3. Lack of adequate funding for important programs and innovation in the immediately ensuing years stifled creativity and encouraged a defensive posture that is occasionally evident even now.

4. Postponement of decisions about marginal programs is unwise. In times of financial crisis, their problems are exacerbated, and they consume valuable resources.

5. Most crises ought not be the surprises that they often are. A modest investment in institutional research and planning is important in developing an advance warning system. Unfortunately, some institutions view these resources as expendable.

Some campuses took the last of these observations seriously, however. For the first time, management concepts were openly pursued and resources were allocated for the purpose of collecting and analyzing data. Colleges overcame their reluctance to exchange with one another information previously considered too sensitive to share. Groups of comparison colleges were established for the purpose of identifying norms, measuring performance, and determining trends. These colleges discovered that they had the capacity—within limits, to be sure—to set goals and take control of their futures.

The Strategic Plan

During the 1984–85 and 1985–86 academic years, Franklin and Marshall undertook an intensive planning venture that included an analysis of the educational program, support services, student flow, and financial parameters; collection of planning information, including general environmental data and comparison data from peer colleges; development of a consensus on mission and goals for the college; and agreement on the major objectives to be accomplished within the first five-year period of the plan. This work formed the basis for the college's first formal strategic plan.

We were reassured by the fact that, on most input and outcome measures, our student indicators fit comfortably with those of our peer colleges. However, it was clear that we were less well endowed than the others, our tuition was below the median, and our annual gift program was less productive. Overall, we were relatively poor among this group of colleges. Implications drawn from environmental data were frightening. We discovered, for example, that, if demographic trends were to drive our admissions outcomes, we could expect an enrollment drop of over 25 percent by fall 1994. Although we had long since begun to broaden our admissions market activity, that work immediately took on a new urgency. We discovered also that our enrollment was high among our peer colleges, we were less residential, and our student-faculty ratio was considerably larger.

As we addressed the matter of institutional vision, we noted that, among liberal arts colleges, Franklin and Marshall is characterized as a research college—where good teaching is fully complemented by a universal commitment to scholarship—with a strong academic program in liberal education. Our faculty are strongly dedicated to teaching, actively engaged in research and creative scholarly activity, and committed to student involvement in independent study. This consensus on institutional vision and a determination to protect and improve the core academic program guided the decisions and planning that followed.

Of the various objectives that we set for ourselves, several are relevant to the discussion here. We first developed a comprehensive, computer-based projection model that permitted us to test those scenarios of particular interest. It became clear to us that we had a mismatch between resources—faculty, facilities, and endowment—and enrollment. The cost of expanding the operating budget and increasing facilities just to reach a student-faculty ratio of 12:1 was disheartening, and the demographic trends made such a response very risky. We were led, therefore, to investigate the consequences of a smaller enrollment, and, to our surprise, this turned out to be a viable option.

Consequently, faculty, and subsequently the trustees, approved a decision to reduce the size of our student body following energetic discussion in the early stages of our counterintuitive approach. The planned reduction was accomplished simply by changing the nominal freshman class size objective from 540 to 475 students beginning, after a false start in 1987, with fall 1988. That turned out to be a propitious time to make such a change.

In fiscal year 1991–1992, the revised class size has had its full effect on overall enrollment, though it is somewhat higher than we originally planned partly as a result of improved retention. Nevertheless, a modest increase in faculty size by 6, to 146, assisted us in achieving a student-faculty ratio slightly below our objective of 12:1. Endowment per student increased by 63 percent to $52,000, and we experienced a more comfortable fit within our facilities.

In many ways, the consequences of the plan have exceeded our expectations and put the college in a strong competitive position. We did not avoid new construction; during this time, we built a new residence hall and a science library, and a new athletic and recreational facility is in the advanced design stages. Also, we did not escape the consequences of the revenue diet and the necessity for reallocation of resources.

General Repositioning Strategies

So that there is no misunderstanding, we acknowledge from the beginning that repositioning means the withdrawal of resources from some program areas of the college so that they can be reallocated elsewhere. We also acknowledge that, unless the institution has been extravagant in its funding of programs, the implication of withdrawal of funds from a particular program is a reduction in that program, either in its scope, level of activity, or both. When demands on the professional and support staff are already high, it is not reasonable or fair to expect the same amount of activity after resources have been reduced. Finally, since employee compensation is typically half of a college's budget, material reallocations of resources require a combination of reassignment and termination of employees accompanied by a careful assessment and, perhaps, reallocation of positions vacated by voluntary retirements and resignations. Although good planning and coordination may reduce the number of employee terminations unrelated to poor performance, the magnitude of the effort and the relatively short time frame for repositioning inevitably lead to some terminations of this kind.

We have applied successfully a number of general principles during the last several years that colleges might consider as they develop plans for repositioning or retrenchment:

Reduce Management Complexity. During growth periods, colleges have the opportunity to divide responsibilities among greater numbers of managers, and there is value in this strategy. Greater attention can be paid to detail, and important program improvements can be realized. At Franklin and Marshall, for example, the student life program was a beneficiary of the growth period, and student advising and retention improved greatly. However, an increase in the number of managers is a costly tactic, implying increases in support staff, office space, equipment, and support services. Communications among management areas become more complex and burdensome. Individual areas may appear to be functioning better, even when the college is not. When revenues are constrained, colleges have a reason other than the exercise of good management practice to reevaluate their management structures, reduce complexity, and release valuable resources. This is not an act of nostalgia, however, and the resulting structure is certain to be different from that of the past.

Eliminate Redundancy. Managers usually prefer to control as much as possible the functions that contribute to their success, at least their perceived success, as managers. Consequently, they may be tempted to duplicate functions or equipment that are available elsewhere, often with small net gains in productivity. Once the commitment is made to duplicate the function, staffing levels tend to be determined by peak period loads. To the extent such redundancy exists, its elimination can generate savings with little loss to the academic program.

Evaluate Every Vacancy. Control of the hiring gate offers the college president an effective and direct way to manage costs. Key questions relating to vacancies are as follows: Must the position be filled? Must it be filled at this level? What opportunities for reconfiguration of tasks does it offer? Occasionally, vacancies need not be filled; we have had persons tell us candidly and accurately in exit interviews that the positions they held were underutilized. Further, college administrators tend to be expansive in developing position descriptions. The complexity and scope of the task are often overstated to ensure that the position is filled at the highest possible salary, educational level, and employee category. This tendency probably arises from the absolute commitment to excellence that we bring to the faculty hiring process, where it is more readily justified. However, application of the same principle to other appointments is expensive, unnecessary, and, in some cases, arguably counter-productive for when we appoint persons with greater aspirations and experience than the position truly requires, unhappy outcomes are likely. It is better to be honest from the beginning regarding the true nature of a position.

Purchase Services Externally. Selective liberal arts colleges are outstanding in their capacity to offer their students a fine education that prepares them for productive, successful, and satisfying lives. Nevertheless, colleges must resist the temptation to think of themselves as inherently superior managers of all conceivable activities. There is even evidence to the contrary. One does not have to control operational detail in order to control the quality of service, and this is particularly true when the service environment is competitive. Given the political nature of the decision process, college administrators often cannot take a bottom-line approach to providing services. Unless compensation policies are market-based, personnel costs are likely to become relatively high. Services provided in-house are often viewed as free by their customer departments. In the competitive environment in which an independent business operates, however, it must be efficient and produce quality work to survive. Finally, in our evaluation of services, we must guard against an overzealous commitment to quality at any cost. Although we may be good at teaching economics, we are not always ready to apply the wisdom that it offers, for example, the law of diminishing returns.

Reallocate Capital Resources. Colleges must learn to manage the use of space more effectively and efficiently, for we never seem to have enough. The cost of space and invested funds, such as inventories, are often ignored in analyzing the costs of operations. Although it is probably not useful for colleges to develop comprehensive chargeback systems, we cannot afford to ignore these costs when we evaluate alternatives.

Reexamine Operating Assumptions. When financial constraints are severe and persistent, colleges must systematically reexamine the fundamental assumptions that inform the budget process, especially those that materially affect revenues and expense. Need-blind admissions is a laudable goal, but the cost appears to be increasing at an unsustainable rate both in terms of numbers of students admitted with financial need and the amount of that need. Colleges may be forced to reexamine average faculty course loads, student-faculty ratios, and class sizes. Endowment spending rates may have to be increased temporarily to the point that real growth in market value comes only through new gifts. Strict congruence of annual adjustments to salaries and fringe benefits with long-term goals may have to be suspended temporarily. Fund-raising goals may have to be revised so as to place greater emphasis on annual current gifts.

Administrative Reward Structure. It is time that colleges reconsider the manner in which senior administrators are rewarded. Rather than focus principally on outcomes, for example, performance analysis should take into account resources consumed in meeting noncurricular objectives. As Maydew (this volume) points out, this is an area in which efficiency must be strongly emphasized.

Assess Programs. Discussion of this topic is relegated to this final position in sequence not because it is relatively unimportant but because, for some colleges, it is among the last considered. Fortunately, a few colleges, such as Bryn Mawr (Pew Higher Education Research Program, 1991), that have realigned programs within the context of their missions have been willing to share their experiences. Colleges find it difficult to think in terms of specific limited program objectives, in part because of the freedom of range of interest and involvement that we give to our faculties, a practice that often leads to the identification of new programs. Long-standing programs are permitted to continue regardless of whether the original need remains. We often pretend that programs are self-supporting when we know they are not, ascribe to them great intangible but unmeasurable benefits, and ask who will do this if we do not—after all, we have been educated in the analytical tradition. Nevertheless, we must ask the difficult questions: Regardless of their intrinsic value to society, how important are these activities to the central mission of the college? How many tuition, gift, and endowment dollars and how much space are we willing to allocate to subsidize them?

Examples of Reallocation Opportunities

When we first explored the consequences of a planned reduction in enrollment at Franklin and Marshall, our principal objective was a continuation of the status quo expenditure base, and projections were based on that assumption. However, colleges cannot operate over the long term on a status quo basis if they are to remain dynamic and vital educational institutions, and, in any case, projection models rarely agree with reality. Funds must be found for innovation, program nourishment, and change. Because we were impatient for action on objectives that arose through academic planning processes, the period of managed enrollment decline was also a time when program budgets increased. We deliberately slowed our progress toward reaching the peer college median for student fees because of our wish to provide parents some relief from the high rates of increase characteristic of the decade. Only recently have we organized to reach our annual fund objectives. Further, we adopted a more conservative endowment cash flow than we assumed in our projections because of the beneficial long-term effect on market values and the extra measure of safety that it provides. Finally, maintenance of a competitive position on faculty compensation has been somewhat more expensive than we anticipated. Since we are obligated to have positive operating margins, our only alternative has been to reallocate resources.

Major changes have been made in the organization of the administration. The number of vice presidents has been reduced by one and the associated responsibilities redistributed, thereby producing additional staff and equipment savings. The number of reporting lines to senior administrators has been reduced by reassigning additional responsibilities further down the hierarchy. Coordination of services and communications has improved noticeably, and this aspect of the reorganization has been enhanced by the appointment of (advisory) administrative working groups established for the purpose of encouraging a creative, broad-based environment for problem solving that does not interfere with the decision process. These working groups also serve to reinforce the notion that administrative offices are not independently functioning entities. Rather, they must operate cooperatively in support of the educational mission of the college. One senior directorship was eliminated, and several administration and staff positions were eliminated following resignations and retirements. The custodial work force has been reorganized into teams involving fewer employees. Of course, as part of this work, numerous positions have been revised and reassigned.

The print shop was for many years a problem area for management. Priorities were always difficult to establish among widely varying publication needs. Although first-in/first-out seemed fair, it did not always make sense if one had the opportunity to intervene; on the other hand, intervention produced a new set of political difficulties. Although the college, by policy, was attempting to accurately charge direct costs to departments using the services, there were numerous times when the system was circumvented, and some departments received favored treatment not at all related to college priorities. Probably because they acquiesced, senior administrators were frequently called on to settle disputes. The college was regularly asked to replace or add equipment. No effort was made to assign indirect costs (for example, fringe benefits, rent, utilities, equipment depreciation, and administrative overhead) to projects, and, had the effort been made, the operation would not have been price competitive with the local market. The quality was generally high, as might be imagined. One solution, of course, would have been for us to start over. However, the many excellent printers in the area offered us the opportunity to close the print shop entirely, eliminate three positions, and recover a portion of the investment in printing equipment with no adjustments to publications budgets. We realized additional savings through the change from a quarterly alumni magazine to a bimonthly tabloid (which, incidentally, is more promptly and widely read) and a publication size more appropriate for mailing. The space recovered, which was in our central services facility, allowed us to complete an expansion and redesign of the college's central air-conditioning system at 20 percent of the originally estimated $1.3 million expense.

For many decades, Franklin and Marshall operated a continuing education program, which, at one time, was the only major program of its kind operating in the area. Courses were different from those taught in the residential program, and, to remain viable, a much lower fee structure was necessary. In recent years, relatively few of our regular faculty taught in this program, since the demands that the residential program places on faculty are great and the continuing education program was, in the view of most, an unwelcome competitor for faculty time. The revenue generated was marginal when all of the usually ignored "overhead" factors were considered; there was increasing competition from other institutions, which ensured availability of educational opportunity; and the program was only marginally distinctive. Therefore, the program and all managerial and staffing responsibilities were moved to the control of another academic institution with a strong commitment to such programs. The program will continue to be offered on a lease basis in Franklin and Marshall facilities, so the community will enjoy what turns out to be an expanded continuing education program at the bachelor's and master's levels. The college continues to benefit from a greater revenue stream without many of the concomitant distractions and administrative burdens of operating a small, isolated program.

As a consequence of several favorable land acquisitions adjacent to the campus, Franklin and Marshall reevaluated all of its property holdings and, subsequently, identified a block of rental properties that were only marginally productive financially and no longer served strategic college needs. An important aspect of real estate investment is appreciation, which is of limited benefit if the owner insists on retaining the property. These properties were sold at greatly appreciated values, subject to right of first refusal on subsequent resales, and restricted to use as single-family dwellings. The neighborhood has benefited from this change, and the college recovered investment control of over $600,000.

One way in which colleges might improve their operating environments is through alternative revenue sources. Franklin and Marshall has established several subsidiary corporations, one of which is a for-profit corporation operating its own facility, free to engage competitively with other businesses in the area. Related to this venture, we have been following discussions at the national and state levels regarding the stance that governments will take vis-à-vis college bookstores. Although we hold the view that the typical college bookstore closely supports the academic program, it is not clear that view will prevail. Now that the issue has been raised, it is natural to ask whether the community will support a university-style bookstore and whether an experienced firm is willing to take on that challenge. Franklin and Marshall found such a firm, sold the college's inventory, thereby recovering investment control of approximately $1 million, eliminated seven positions from its payroll, and now offers under the aegis of the for-profit subsidiary access to a much larger inventory than was previously possible. As is often the case on campuses, the bookstore was in the centrally located college center; we will soon open a fine art gallery in the vacated space.

In summary, these actions, along with energy conservation projects, produced the following approximate financial results in 1991 dollars: annual operating savings, $1,242,000; capital funds recovered, $2,645,000; and avoided short-term capital expense, $1,000,000.

General Observations

Franklin and Marshall has long enjoyed a reputation of operating with a relatively lean expenditure base. It is with great trepidation that one approaches repositioning under such circumstances, for there are no obvious reductions to be made. When this issue arises in discussions among other college presidents and vice presidents, the conversation often begins with a declaration that there simply is not any place to make reductions without harming programs. While that interpretation may be valid in some sense, it is of little help. Nearly every institution has choices as to how expenditure reductions might be made, and some reductions are more harmful than others. The challenge is to minimize the damage to the programs central to the college's mission. In our case, there certainly were discernible changes, and the greatest of these are most evident in administrative functions: There are fewer opportunities to delegate work, loss of the print shop makes printing less convenient, and some tasks can no longer be undertaken. Documents that once were professionally printed are now produced on the laser printer and copied. Members of the surrounding community liked having Franklin and Marshall's name on their continuing education transcripts, but under the new arrangement they are likely to be taking the same courses taught by the same people. Residence halls will still be cleaned, but custodians will not be available on call as they were previously.

Approximately thirty positions have been removed from the college payroll as a consequence of the reallocations and reductions described above. The net number of reductions is less, of course, because we deliberately set out to reallocate resources within our planned expenditure base. In some cases, we were able to maintain employment for persons displaced by these actions, but in new areas. Others were able to fill vacancies occurring as a consequence of normal turnover. Finally, however, there were some persons who could not be accommodated in this manner, and, sadly, there were no mutually acceptable options we could offer.

The steps we have described are intended as examples, not a prescription to be followed by other colleges. Purchase of services from outside the institution is not always the answer. Some institutions have contracted externally for security services, but, because of the manner in which our office of safety and security relates to residential programs, we do not see contracting out as an attractive direction for us at this time. Our physical plant operation works well, so we are not inclined to favor the external management option. We contract externally for custodial services in educational and office buildings, but, after careful consideration, we have elected not to do so for our residence halls. For colleges with missions substantially different from ours, continuing education programs may be inextricably intertwined with their residential programs and provide an important revenue stream. Each institution must find its own way through the maze, but perhaps some guidance may be gained through the experience of others wrestling with similar kinds of problems.

We must acknowledge that there are times when major problems arise with little apparent advance warning. On such occasions, an institution may be faced with the inescapable choice of taking stopgap actions—severe reductions in already approved budgets, hiring freezes, faculty and staff layoffs, salary freezes, and so on—or watching the negative impact of the financial reversal grow. Decisions must be made quickly as to the nature and extent of remedies if precious financial reserves are not to be wasted. In these times, hasty action can cause great damage if a more carefully crafted, longer-term response is not soon forthcoming. A strong, broad-based institutional research and planning capability immediately accessible to senior administrators is of great value as options are sought, identified, and evaluated. Because it is essentially impossible to build that capability in times of crisis, we cannot overemphasize the importance of maintaining a functioning institutional research and planning office at all times. This resource offers the additional advantage of reducing the number of unanticipated major crises that an institution must face.

In conclusion, we can confidently state that as a consequence of the actions we have taken, the academic program at Franklin and Marshall College is stronger than it otherwise would have been, and we can assuredly plan for additional improvements in the future even though the economic climate may force us to move more slowly than we would wish in their implementation.

References

Cage, M. C. "30 States Cut Higher-Education Budgets by an Average of 3.9% in Fiscal 1990–91." *Chronicle of Higher Education,* June 26, 1991, pp. A1, A17.

Cheit, E. *The New Depression in Higher Education.* New York: McGraw-Hill, 1971.

Pew Higher Education Research Program. "Bryn Mawr College: Achieving Financial Equilibrium." *Policy Perspectives,* 1991, 3 (2), 14B–15B.

Zemsky, R., and Massy, W. F. "Cost Containment: Committing to a New Economic Reality." *Change,* 1990, 22 (6), 16–22.

Zemsky, R., and Massy, W. F. "The Other Side of the Mountain." *Policy Perspectives,* 1991, 3 (2), 1A–8A.

RICHARD B. HOFFMAN, vice president and chief financial officer at Franklin and Marshall College, Lancaster, Pennsylvania, is also a lecturer in physics and serves as a member of the board of the Higher Education Data Sharing Consortium.

Total Quality Management teaches how to study and improve an institution's processes, thereby improving both quality and productivity.

Total Quality Management: Increasing Productivity and Decreasing Costs

Mary Ann Heverly, Robert A. Cornesky

Total Quality Management (TQM) is a philosophy of improving quality by ceaselessly improving the processes that support the mission of an organization. In contrast to the traditional management assumption that quality improvements are associated with increased costs, TQM teaches that continuous process improvement enhances productivity and lowers costs. This chapter delineates the basic worldview that informs TQM and examines how productivity and quality costs are assessed in the TQM model. It also illustrates how colleges and universities are using TQM to increase productivity and reduce costs and addresses the application of TQM to the research and planning functions of colleges and universities.

Philosophy of Total Quality Management

Although TQM has helped to transform the economy of Japan and is now being adopted by other countries as they face the increasingly competitive world market, its roots can be traced to America, where Walter Shewhart, working at Bell Laboratories, developed the concepts and tools that underlie modern statistical quality control. These methods and tools were so valuable during World War II that they were classified by the government until the war had ended (Ishikawa, 1985).

W. Edwards Deming taught these methods to the Japanese after the war; Deming, Joseph Juran, and other quality experts gradually came to realize that quality control could not be relegated to a distinct quality-control department. Rather, the philosophy, concepts, and methods had to be assimilated by the entire organization and supported by the commitment of executive staff (Ishikawa, 1985).

Quality improvement sets in motion a sequence of events that includes increases in productivity and decreases in cost, with the ultimate effects of increased market share and a positive return on investment. This sequence is known as the Deming Chain Reaction (Deming, 1986), and it contradicts the worldview of most American managers, who assume that the cost of investing in quality improvement will eventually outweigh any return on investment. To understand how TQM arrives at such a different perspective, one needs to understand its basic underlying principles.

Basic Principles. TQM requires a long-term view because its implementation takes time and effort. It is not a "quick fix" solution, and a significant part of the return on investment will emerge only in long-term analysis of an institution's functioning. To adopt Total Quality as a management style, managers must surrender their obsession with short-term productivity and cost analyses.

TQM emphasizes an institution's processes, not its products or outcomes. Processes are identified and studied, and data are gathered to understand how the processes are operating. The goal is to continuously improve processes, because a better process yields better outcomes. This approach is preventive in nature. It identifies characteristics of a process that lead to inefficiencies or to unwanted results, and it reduces inefficiencies by preventing those characteristics.

The traditional approach to quality emphasizes the results (products or outcomes) of processes and invests heavily in inspecting these results. Inspection is a post hoc activity focused on fixing or discarding outcomes that do not meet specifications. Inspection does not prevent problems and is more costly than prevention. However, prevention's cost advantage does not appear unless a long-term view is adopted.

Most American managers focus exclusively on outcomes. They set quantitative goals for their employees and fail to take time to study the processes that produce outcomes. This tendency exists in industry (where outcomes may be automobiles or computer chips), in service organizations (where outcomes may be loans awarded or patients treated), and in education (where outcomes may be students graduated or students placed in jobs).

On the surface, a focus on outcomes appears to be a reasonable approach. What could possibly be wrong with it? In fact, it ignores the needs of customers, fails to take advantage of the gains that could be made by studying the processes in an organization, and fuels employee resentment, frustration, and fear (Scholtes, 1990). This focus on numerical outcomes, which distorts the system and generates unwanted and unanticipated costs throughout the system, has been termed the "perversity principle" (Tribus and Tsuda, 1985, p. 35).

In addition to long-term thinking and a process orientation, TQM requires a commitment to identifying the customers of a process and studying their needs. Outcome measures are not eliminated or ignored in

TQM; on the contrary, data are gathered on *both* process and outcomes. The key is to identify appropriate outcome measures by conducting research on customer needs.

Measurement Implications. TQM requires that management decisions be data-driven and that measures be developed to assess the quality of the process as well as the quality of the product or service generated by the process. Imai (1986, p. 39) refers to these two types of measures as "p" (process) criteria and "r" (results) criteria, respectively. Most organizations have a tradition of gathering data on "r" criteria; data gathering on the process is a less common practice. This tradition is unfortunate because measures of "p" criteria often provide a greater opportunity for productivity gains and cost savings.

The importance of process measures is illustrated by Fuller's (1985) distinction between "real work" in a process and "complexity." Real work is composed of the activities and steps in a process that add value to the output (product or service) of the process. Complexity is composed of the activities or steps in a process that add no value to the output. Examples of complexity include unnecessary steps, errors, and rework (doing things over or fixing mistakes). When Fuller gathered data on the actual time spent on real work, he found that the proportion was 43 percent in a factory setting and 35 percent in a marketing office. In other words, unnecessary tasks and rework consumed over half of available staff time in both settings.

Implications: Training and Education. Implementation of TQM requires that an organization make a firm and enduring commitment to educating staff in the Total Quality philosophy, methods, and tools. Opportunities and incentives for putting the method to actual use must be provided. The effort demands a substantial investment of resources, but if the institution maintains its commitment to implementing TQM, the time and effort eventually will be allocated across a continuing stream of improvement projects, both large and small, and will continue to improve both efficiency and effectiveness.

Motorola University, founded by Motorola to improve the basic skills of its work force and to educate the work force about quality, commissioned a study of the return on investment of this effort (Wiggenhorn, 1990). The results varied according to the degree to which TQM had been adopted. If employees had assimilated the concepts and were encouraged by managers to use the tools, the return on investment was $33 per $1 invested. If either the process focus or the quality tools was adopted by employees and supported by managers, the breakeven point was reached. If the curriculum had been taught but there were no follow-up efforts to ensure on-the-job applications, the return on investment was negative. The lesson drawn by the company was that top management had to drive the transformation, not merely give it lip service.

How Total Quality Management Defines and Measures Quality Costs

TQM's model of evaluating costs is derived from the statistical quality-control literature. Quality costs are split into two categories: the *costs of control* and the *costs of failure* to control (Feigenbaum, 1983). The costs of control include all of the activities that are directed at improving quality. The costs of failure to control include the costs of all of the inefficiencies in processes and the costs of ineffectiveness in meeting customers' needs. This view forces managers to quantify complexity in processes and to tie outcome measures to customer needs.

Costs of Improving Quality. Feigenbaum (1983) separates the costs of improving quality, that is, the costs of control, into two components: *prevention costs* and *appraisal costs*. Prevention costs are the costs of working upstream to improve the process. They include resources spent on staff education about quality, quality planning, process control, and the design and development of process and results measures. Appraisal costs are the costs of assessing the product or service generated by processes. They include the traditional quality-control costs of conducting testing, inspection, assessment, evaluations, and audits.

Costs of Failure to Control Quality. These two types of costs also have two components: *costs of internal failure* and *costs of external failure*. Internal failure refers to errors, rework, and other forms of complexity detected by the organization's appraisal system. An education example would be a student's failure in a course and the requirement to take it a second time. External failure occurs when a mistake (or any poor-quality product or service) is not detected by the appraisal system and reaches a customer. (The customer could be an external customer served by the institution, or the customer could be a staff member who is an "internal" customer of the process.)

Some features of internal and external failure costs can be quantified and assigned monetary values; others remain unknown (Deming, 1986). For example, staff time spent correcting errors detected by an internal checking system, or resources expended to handle customer problems, can be assessed and translated into monetary terms. However, the most damaging results of internal and external failures cannot always be quantified. The real cost of a dissatisfied customer is an unknown parameter (Deming, 1986). Latzko (1986) points out that this principle extends to the effects on employees who, as internal customers of processes within the organization, are recipients of internal failures. Latzko warns that these unmeasured costs are so significant that the proper approach for a Total Quality manager is to focus on profits, not costs. In the nonprofit sector, this translates into a focus on satisfying the customers of a process.

How Quality Improvement Decreases Costs. Feigenbaum (1983) describes the mechanisms that yoke quality to improved productivity and decreased cost. Table 8.1 shows Feigenbaum's assessment of how quality costs are distributed in industry, as well as Latzko's assessment for part of the service sector (banking). The table reveals that the costs of failure (both internal and external) constitute the largest proportion of total quality costs, while the costs of prevention represent the smallest proportion. The effect of prevention efforts is to reduce both internal and external failure costs. Feigenbaum points out that prevention efforts also tend to reduce appraisal costs because a properly operating process creates fewer defects or problems to be inspected. In other words, an ounce of prevention is worth a pound of cure.

How does the traditional approach to quality and costing reach the opposite conclusion about quality and productivity? The traditional management approach to improving quality is to increase appraisal (inspection) costs (Feigenbaum, 1983). Inspection has several disadvantages. It is costly, accounting for about a quarter of total quality costs. Unlike prevention, inspection activities do not address the source of failures; they simply sort outcomes into "acceptable" and "not acceptable" piles. Unlike prevention, inspection does not generate reductions in the costs of internal and external failures. As just noted, it does not address internal failures at all. Nor is it very effective in reducing the external failure toward which it is directed. One hundred percent inspection does not eliminate defects; some continue to reach the customer. Feigenbaum (1983) reports that responding to high external failure rates by putting resources into appraisal usually has the paradoxical result of increasing *both* appraisal costs and external failure costs.

Applying Total Quality Management to Higher Education

Education in the United States has been facing crises on multiple fronts: long-standing nationwide concern over the quality of education, budgetary restrictions at every level of government and in every region of the

Table 8.1. Estimated Percentage Distributions of Quality Costs: Industrial and Service Sectors

Quality Costs	Industrial	Service
Failure costs	65–70	70[a]
Appraisal costs	20–25	28
Prevention costs	5–10	2

[a] 41 percent internal failure, 29 percent external failure costs.

Sources: Feigenbaum, 1983 (industrial data); Latzko, 1986 (service data).

country, and increasingly strident calls from stakeholders for educational institutions to document their worth. In times of crisis, when organizations are driven to identify solutions to pressing problems, they can become more receptive to change. During the 1980s, many American businesses turned to TQM as a means of retaining or regaining a competitive position in the marketplace. During the last half decade, businesses in the service sector, nonprofit organizations, and government agencies have adopted TQM to help them run more efficiently in a time of diminishing resources. Although education has lagged behind in exploring TQM, a groundswell of interest is emerging as executives and administrators seek new and better ways to conduct their enterprise.

Most institutions interested in TQM are in the early learning stages. Data on productivity and cost reductions effected by TQM are emerging slowly because it takes time to develop the new ways of thinking and to adopt and apply the new methods and tools. Nevertheless, a few examples of productivity and cost studies in a TQM context are available, and some of these are described below.

Institutionwide Cost Analysis. Spanbauer (1989) has described the costing methods developed to assess institutionwide quality costs at Fox Valley Technical College. The college followed the model of the American Society for Quality Control. Quality costs are referred to as "conformance costs" and failure costs are referred to as "nonconformance costs."

The Fox Valley model includes the following costs of conformance: market research, quality training for employees, quality coordination, quality monitoring and auditing, and wellness programs. The total costs of conformance for 1987–1988 were $172,059. And the model includes the following costs of nonconformance: proportion of class seats that are filled, service department rework, student attrition, employee absenteeism, suboptimal scheduling of staff members, and customer service. (The latter is the euphemism American organizations use for customer complaint and return departments.) The total cost of nonconformance in 1987–1988 was $8,124,270. Total quality costs (conformance and nonconformance) were $8,296,329. Note that the cost of conformance is 2 percent of total quality costs. This estimate closely matches the relative cost of prevention estimated for industrial and for service companies (see Table 8.1). A closer look at Spanbauer's list of conformance cost activities reveals that they represent predominantly prevention activities. Thus, independent analyses from different sectors yield similar estimates of the percentage of total quality costs represented by prevention.

The operational definitions of these components are detailed by Spanbauer (1989). At Fox Valley, nonconformance costs are defined as the expense of *any* deviation from 100 percent efficiency. Spanbauer notes that even though perfection may be an unattainable goal, the use of this standard reveals to staff the cost of failing to improve processes. In

1987–1988, the cost of rework was calculated as 20 percent of a service department's budget, an estimate that uses the lower end of most quality experts' estimated range of rework costs. Fox Valley is currently tabulating the actual costs of rework.

Administrative Productivity and Cost Analyses. Institutions seeking to implement TQM often begin in the administrative arena. One reason is that similar administrative functions exist in other types of organizations more experienced in using TQM. Consequently, examples of comparable applications and models of implementation exist in the quality literature. Also, the first persons to become interested in TQM often are administrators, and it is natural to begin practicing on processes that "belong" to the practitioner.

Coate (1990) has reported on productivity gains resulting from TQM project team activity at Oregon State University. For example, a team from physical plant studied the process of conducting a remodeling project, implemented changes based on the data, and reduced the average cycle time by 23 percent. Another team studied a problem with unanswered employee phone calls to the office handling staff benefits. Study of the process led to improvements that boosted answered calls by 40 percent and reduced staff time in the benefits office spent on these calls (from 35 percent to 1 percent). The improvements reaped the additional benefit of reduced complaints from internal customers (employees). As previously observed, failures that create customer dissatisfaction are costly; although their actual cost is unmeasured, what is known is that the effects are multiple and negative and reverberate throughout the processes of an organization (Goodman, Malech, and Marra, 1987).

In conducting cost studies, it is especially important to maintain the focus on process, for it is in conducting productivity and cost analyses that the gravitational pull toward short-term, bottom-line, results-oriented management is strongest. If a manager loses sight of the process data, the most significant impact of a quality-improvement effort may be missed. The importance of the process focus is illustrated by an example from a team studying the photocopying system at Delaware County Community College. The team was created in response to widespread dissatisfaction with the copiers in administrative and instructional areas. Data gathered on the process and from customers led to the development of a new system for copying in the college. The team reported on a variety of "r" and "p" measures taken before and after the new system was implemented. The "r" measures showed some changes in the desired direction—for example, the volume of copying had been a concern and it dropped by over 400,000 copies in the first nine months of 1989–1990 (compared to the same time frame in 1987–1988). However, if this were the only effect of the team's work, one might question whether the results justified the expenditure of resources to attain them. The most striking result was a "p" measure—an average daily reduction of 11.5 hours in the time secretaries were spending on photocopying.

Applications in the Instructional Area. The School of Science, Management, and Technologies at Edinboro University of Pennsylvania instituted a series of TQM systems as a result of the long-range plan and resource allocation procedure. The systems approach used various tools, including "fishbone" charts, to encourage faculty and staff to suggest ways to increase efficiency and quality. The fishbone chart (also called a cause-and-effect diagram) is a TQM tool that outlines possible causes of an effect being studied. It focuses and guides data collection and analysis. For example, Figure 8.1 charts the perceptions of faculty in the School of Science, Management, and Technologies as to why an insufficient number of general education courses were scheduled (heavy horizontal line). Long and short diagonal lines show cause-and-effect factors that impinge on problem resolution.

One example of increased efficiency comes from the Mathematics

Figure 8.1 Example of a Fishbone Chart
(Cause and Effect Diagram)

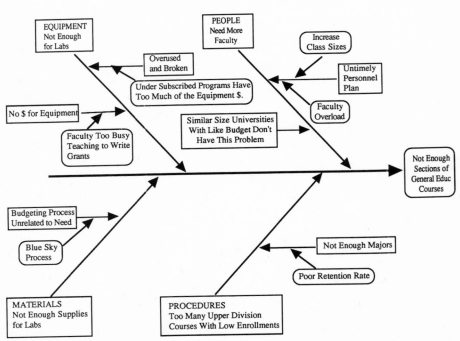

Note: This chart outlines the perceptions of the faculty in the School of Science, Management, and Technologies about why an insufficient number of general education courses were scheduled.

and Computer Science Department. The chair noted that students dropping out of classes in a required computer science course generated thirty-six empty seats every semester. The chair withdrew students who missed the first several classes and filled the seats with students from a waiting list.

Fishbone charts also helped to improve the quality of services to students. Charts were posted in places that were high-traffic areas for targeted groups. For example, a chart citing a perceived problem (negative attitudes toward students) was placed in the Dean's Office so that students could list what they perceived to be major causes. As a result, faculty, staff, and administration made a serious effort to be more sensitive to the needs of the customer.

Fishbone charts identifying another problem (poor ratings of professors by students) were placed in several departmental offices. The responses from faculty led to a suggested revision of the faculty evaluation procedure.

Before TQM was adopted, department chairs assumed that the major problems with improving faculty performance and morale were due to management-union antagonism and an incompetent and vindictive administration. Perceived counterbalances to these problems were the strengths of a committed faculty and solid academic programs. After one year of instituting the long-range plan and resource allocation procedure and studying and adopting TQM, a nominal group process revealed that chairs saw the following problems to be primary: lack of facilities, timeliness of administrative decisions, poor student profiles, micromanagement by administration, and uncommitted faculty. It is noteworthy that the management-union relationship was ranked tenth. In addition, one dimension perceived as an institutional strength in the prior year—level of faculty commitment—was now perceived as a major weakness.

After two years of refining and instituting the long-range plan and TQM, the School of Science, Management, and Technologies chairs perceived the following to inhibit quality: inefficient management systems, lack of funds for classrooms and offices, unstable base of resources, and inability to attract quality faculty. That is, after two years, the "we versus them" (union versus administration) feeling was not perceived as the problem. The problem, as perceived by the chairs, was not with the people but with the processes and systems. Adoption of the TQM philosophy means admitting that things are wrong, so that progress can be made to improve processes and systems. Although solid academic programs initially were perceived as a strength, in two years every program had been substantially or completely revised.

As a result of the new openness, several faculty members began to experiment with different teaching methods: teleclasses, videocourses, team projects, case studies, inquiry methods, and discussion. The experiments were presented at an academic festival and provided ideas for future research. Faculty became interested and attended seminars on teaching-learning styles and syllabus preparation.

Training in the new approach enabled secretaries to make recommendations that streamlined routine office procedures. Secretaries in the School of Science, Management, and Technologies participated in TQM workshops, both on campus and off campus. In addition, many audio- and videotaped programs were purchased to help the secretaries develop their skills and abilities. As a result of training, the secretaries participated in a nominal group process that identified five major problems: lack of job training, poor communications within and among departments, negative attitudes, lack of collegiality, and inability to effect change.

Fishbone charts identifying lack of job training as the problem were posted for secretaries to use in identifying causes. The most common causes identified were the following: no orientation, inaccurate job description, no input from faculty as to expectations, no office procedure training, no encouragement by administration, and lack of combined workshops on teaming for faculty, secretaries, and administration. Every issue is being addressed. Several secretaries have reported a feeling of pride in their work, stemming from this trust and empowerment. Other case studies and examples are provided in Cornesky (1990) and Cornesky, McCool, Byrnes, and Weber (1991). There has been progress in resolving several issues that inhibited quality instruction and performance; faculty and staff have become more vocal and are willing to risk change and innovation in an effort to improve quality.

Implications for Institutional Research. TQM is based on the premise that work can be conducted more efficiently and effectively without requiring additional resources. The goal of improving the effectiveness of institutional research requires thoroughly understanding the needs of customers who use the products (reports, summaries) and services (provision of information or assistance) of institutional research. Most are internal customers, people who depend on institutional research's products and services to conduct their own work. Although the concept of needs assessment is well known to researchers, the practice of systematically gathering data to assess the needs of internal customers is not common. TQM begins with data gathering on customer requirements, operational definitions of these requirements as measures, and data gathering on these measures to determine how well the requirements are being met, that is, how effective the processes are in delivering what the customers need. Efficiency is improved by gathering data on the processes in order to bring to light areas of rework or complexity. Removal of rework and complexity frees resources that can be directed toward the real work of institutional research.

One way to apply TQM is to focus on a regularly occurring process important to the institution—the process of preparing a specific report or conducting a specific survey, for example. Identify the process inputs, major steps, and outputs. Inputs are the resources (materials, supplies, information) necessary for the process to occur. Process steps are the activities that must occur to complete the process. Outputs of the process may be tangible, such as a written report or document, or intangible, such as information or ideas communicated orally. Next, identify the customers or users of the outputs and their requirements. It may be necessary to gather data on the characteristics they require of the process output.

This initial phase sets the stage for data collection that will guide continuous process improvement. Two types of data are required. The first type of data measures how well the outputs are meeting customer needs. This customer data identifies areas for improvement in the quality of the output (effectiveness). The second type of data measures the process. For example, the frequency of delays, errors, and other problems that occur with inputs and at each step in the process can be recorded to identify areas for process improvement. These process improvements streamline the process and improve efficiency.

Because TQM pushes managers to gather data in a systematic fashion and to use the data, it can facilitate the work of institutional researchers. Institutional researchers engage in a daily struggle to determine the information needs of administrators, faculty, and staff. TQM offers a philosophy that drives everyone in the organization to use data, and it provides methods and tools for achieving this purpose. The potential impact in an institution implementing TQM is profound and far-reaching, eventually transforming it into what Senge (1990) calls a "learning organization." As continuous process improvement becomes an integral part of everyone's daily work, the institutional research function increasingly becomes supportive. The effect is paradoxical; the less that data gathering is seen as the exclusive domain of institutional research, the greater the leverage that institutional research acquires as a facilitator of many more activities than could be conducted within its domain alone.

References

Coate, L. E. *An Analysis of Oregon State University's Total Quality Management Pilot Program.* Corvallis: Oregon State University, 1990.

Cornesky, R. A. *W. Edwards Deming: Improving Quality in Colleges and Universities.* Madison, Wis.: Magna, 1990.

Cornesky, R. A., McCool, S., Byrnes, L., and Weber, R. *Implementing Total Quality Management in Higher Education.* Madison, Wis.: Magna, 1991.

Deming, W. E. *Out of the Crisis.* Cambridge: Center for Advanced Engineering Study, Massachusetts Institute of Technology, 1986.

Feigenbaum, A. V. *Total Quality Control.* (3rd ed.) New York: McGraw-Hill, 1983.
Fuller, F. T. "Eliminating Complexity from Work: Improving Productivity by Enhancing Quality." *National Productivity Review,* 1985, *4,* 327–344.
Goodman, J., Malech, A., and Marra, T. "I Can't Get No Satisfaction." *Quality Review,* 1987, *1* (4), 11–14.
Imai, M. *Kaizen: The Key to Japan's Competitive Success.* New York: Random House, 1986.
Ishikawa, K. *What Is Total Quality Control?* (D. J. Lu, trans.) Englewood Cliffs, N.J.: Prentice Hall, 1985.
Latzko, W. J. *Quality and Productivity for Bankers and Financial Managers.* Milwaukee, Wis.: ASQC Quality Press, 1986.
Scholtes, P. R. *The Team Handbook: How to Use Teams to Improve Quality.* Madison, Wis.: Joiner Associates, 1990.
Senge, P. M. *The Fifth Discipline: The Art and Practice of the Learning Organization.* New York: Doubleday, 1990.
Spanbauer, S. J. *Measuring and Costing Quality in Education.* Appleton, Wis.: Fox Valley Technical College Foundation, 1989.
Tribus, M., and Tsuda, Y. *The Quality Imperative in the New Economic Era.* Cambridge: Center for Advanced Engineering Study, Massachusetts Institute of Technology, 1985.
Wiggenhorn, W. "Motorola U.: When Training Becomes an Education." *Harvard Business Review,* 1990, *68,* 71–83.

MARY ANN HEVERLY is director of institutional research at Delaware County Community College, Media, Pennsylvania.

ROBERT A. CORNESKY, former dean of the School of Science, Management, and Technologies at Edinboro University of Pennsylvania, is a Total Quality Management consultant.

Colleges and universities must commit to long-term solutions to
overcome their fiscal crises.

Where Do We Go from Here?

Carol S. Hollins

The issues of increased costs, decreased productivity, and a perceived decline in quality have hovered over higher education for too long. Few other topics have commanded the attention of public audiences and educators as have the presumed inefficiencies in higher education. In fact, this matter has reverberated among all types of institutions without regard to control, level, or state. When we combine its effects with declining public perception of American higher education and one of the most severe budget crises in recent history, it becomes understandable why there is a general malaise among educators concerning the future.

The authors in this volume have revisited the litany of questions that will not go away, such as "What *are* faculty doing?" "Why is there so much administrative bloat?" "Is there an end to soaring tuition charges?" Everyone knows that college costs have outpaced inflation, but what is more distressing is the claim that students are being shortchanged by unproductive faculty. While such issues are disturbing to those of us in the higher education community, until recently, little has been done to challenge the accusations.

As might be expected, the authors here were not able to disprove the academic ratchet of increased specialization, nor the cost disease that seems indigenous to higher education. In fact, we documented other excesses as well, such as the administrative lattice, output creep, organizational slack, and cost-plus pricing. One positive outcome of our investigation was the opportunity to critically examine these productivity concepts as well as to discover ways to address the current predicament of higher education.

Unfortunately, what the concepts do not convey is the critical need to review assumptions about faculty work load and student-teacher ratios, and to redefine what constitutes work, as pointed out by both Brinkman (Chapter Two) and Hoffman (Chapter Seven). There seems to be a trade-off between teaching and research according to Gilmore and To (Chapter Three). Faculty are responding to pressures to do research, which has diminished teaching time. In fact, findings from a national study revealed that "the more college faculty teach, the less they are paid" (Mooney, 1992). Several institutions have begun a dialogue about this matter in hopes of striking a more appropriate balance between teaching and research. Others are reviewing existing structures that reward scholarship over teaching. Until more institutions are willing to debate this controversial topic and reach a compromise, it will continue to plague us.

Higher Education Costs

We have gone from relatively booming to austere conditions in American higher education in a rather short period of time. Prior to the 1970s, expansion was possible because we had the funds to support comprehensive academic and administrative programs. When federal and state economies were dealt serious blows in the last few years, many of us were still looking for a windfall and instead received a shortfall of epidemic proportions.

It is especially troublesome that we did not recognize what was happening beforehand, as Massy and Zemsky (1990) point out. As a result, because of budget shortages, tuition costs have risen by 2.8 to 2.9 percent annually among public universities and about 3.5 percent among the privates over the consumer price index. Administrative support costs rose by about 60 percent between 1975 and 1985, some of which was beyond our control, but much of which can be credited to increased levels of service, additions, and enhancements to programs, as argued by Maydew (Chapter Four). Middaugh and Hollowell (Chapter Five) point out that the real cost drivers were employee salaries and fringe benefits.

A number of complex factors drive college costs, as detailed by Brinkman. However, in spite of the varied reasons why costs are rising, pressures will continue to be exerted on virtually all institutions to contain costs. When we consider that other agencies and industries are downsizing and eliminating slack, higher education cannot expect to escape pruning. After all, legislators, foundations, parents, and donors are demanding evidence of sound management and budget controls to justify increased expenditures.

Bowen (1980) says that costs rose because educational institutions have an ingrained propensity to accelerate spending in order to achieve their dominant goals of "educational excellence, prestige, and influence." Internal pressures are to increase resources and spending, not to trim back. Massy and Zemsky (1990) refer to it as "the growth force," and they say it is endemic—we in higher education always want to do more. As Dunn (Chapter One) aptly points out, college costs have increased significantly when incomes have not. Clearly, the time has come to contain the costs of higher education within general inflation.

Improved Productivity

In the broadest sense, productivity is the ratio of inputs to outputs. Inputs are relatively easy to define, but academic outcomes are "difficult and diffuse," according to Mingle and Lenth (1989). The often-used analogy of the string quartet has limitations in an educational environment. In labor-intensive organizations, it is much easier to realize qualitative improvements than it is to show quantitative increases.

Nonetheless, several of the authors in this volume acknowledge that organizational slack has built up over the good times, and we must now deal with our excess baggage. Massy and Zemsky's (1990) "propagation of property rights" and "academic ratchet" refer to how things (such as tenure) get entrenched and immobile. They state that the real issue is "output creep," where the winners of this shifting of priorities in higher education have been curriculum specialization and unsponsored research activity, and the losers are structure in the curriculum and the quality of undergraduate teaching. In fact, this is the crux of the matter—an erosion in the quality and attention given to undergraduate teaching. While no one is denying the need to reemphasize teaching at the undergraduate level, few are addressing pressures that faculty face to publish or perish.

The noncurricular side of the house is not without its critics either. Maydew focuses on rising administrative costs and the need for institutions to initiate cost-restraining activities in support areas. There is also a need to critically examine administrative costs over time, as pointed out by Middaugh and Hollowell as well as by Knepp (Chapter Six), to pinpoint specifically where the growth has occurred.

Commitment to Long-Term Solutions

Higher education is at a crossroads of sorts. Where *do* we go from here? Will our institutions be able to survive the severe cost constraints that are being imposed on them? Do we need new, creative ways of funding public higher education? Are we headed toward greater government intervention due to declining public trust? It seems that we have an opportunity to combine a number of cost reductions with productivity improvements, as suggested by the authors in this volume. Several recommendations are summarized below that require a deliberate and long-term commitment by institutions in order to be effective. Obviously, the list is not intended to be prescriptive but to serve as a stimulant for further institutional dialogue.

Reassess Institutional Goals and Priorities. Most of us agree that our institutions cannot be all things to all people. Colleges and universities should take this opportunity to review their overall mission, vision, and values. Extend this process to academic and administrative units. After reaching agreement on major thrusts, seek to develop a common understanding of institutional targets. Communicate often about the need for change. Reduce costs associated with low-priority or marginal activities. Examine high-priority programs and services to ensure cost-effectiveness and integration into the institution's overall mission and goals.

Reallocate or Grow by Substitution. Admittedly, many more changes can be made during a time of financial exigency than can be made otherwise. Growth by substitution allows an institution to be responsive to change and prudent as well. For every new activity, identify an existing one that must be eliminated or curtailed. Every change is an opportunity to reassess. Is there continued demand for our academic and support programs? Are they consistent with the institution's mission and goals? Are they operating efficiently? We should explore other opportunities to streamline by reallocating existing resources.

Streamline Structures and Functions. Where possible, centralize structures and functions to improve quality and reduce costs, especially in small to medium-size institutions. Broaden responsibilities and cross-train to reduce specialization. In some cases, decentralization may work better in large universities to simplify bureaucracy and improve responsiveness. Move decision making down in the organization to the lowest possible level. Diminish complexity and redundancy by reducing layers of management. Streamline organizational structure and create a more integrated focus by combining overlapping functions.

Make Better Use of Technology. Granted the use of technology alone cannot reduce costs. However, we should automate manual processes to realize productivity improvements that would not be possible otherwise. Computers hold a great deal of promise for streamlining tasks that involve repetition and can free up time for other duties.

Explore Total Quality Management (TQM) Programs. As noted by Heverly and Cornesky (Chapter Eight), TQM is not a quick fix solution for our ills. Instead, TQM requires commitment to a long-term analysis of an institution's functioning. TQM has the potential to increase productivity and decrease costs through prevention, not just inspection. Herein lies the potential to focus simultaneously on cost containment and quality improvements.

Invest in Systematic Research and Planning. Establish a well-designed, functional planning process. Commit to ongoing evaluation of administrative and academic functions through systematic research and analysis. Interinstitutional data comparisons are useful to identify norms, assess trends, and conduct meaningful evaluations of institutional effectiveness. Explore long-range planning and budgeting beyond the annual cycle. As Hoffman notes, this is something that cannot be done when an institution is in a crisis mode.

Practice General Frugality. When feasible, purchase services externally. On the other hand, use in-house expertise to complete tasks that might otherwise be contracted out, for example, publications. Examine resources consumed to accomplish noncurricular objectives. Investigate cooperative ventures with other institutions of higher education. Explore multiple uses of the college's physical assets.

A number of persons in the academy are viewing the current fiscal crisis as an aberration and are ready to rebound. This perspective is not surprising; we tend to resist all diets, even revenue diets that require strict discipline to achieve the desired effect. Yet, if we bypass the scrutiny that frugal times afford us, we may miss a unique opportunity to reposition our institution strategically for the next century, an omission that we may live to regret.

References

Bowen, H. R. *The Costs of Higher Education: How Much Do Colleges and Universities Spend Per Student and How Much Should They Spend?* San Francisco: Jossey-Bass, 1980.

Massy, W. F., and Zemsky, R. *The Dynamics of Academic Productivity.* (J. R. Mingle, comp.) Denver, Colo.: State Higher Education Executive Officers, 1990.

Mingle, J. R., and Lenth, C. S. *A New Approach to Accountability and Productivity in Higher Education.* Denver, Colo.: State Higher Education Executive Officers, 1989.

Mooney, C. J. "Syracuse Seeks a Balance Between Teaching and Research." *Chronicle of Higher Education,* Mar. 25, 1992, pp. A1, A14–A16.

CAROL S. HOLLINS is coordinator of institutional research at John Tyler Community College, Chester, Virginia.

INDEX

Academic productivity. *See* Productivity, academic
Academic ratchet, 1, 2, 21, 61, 117
Administration: and cost constraints, 9; cost-effectiveness of, 51–56; increased cost of, 116; norms of, as cost factor, 27–28; productivity of, 49–51; reducing cost of, 50–51, 56–58. *See also* Personnel; Productivity, administrative; Staff
Administrative lattice, 1, 2, 28, 61
Alpert, D., 27
Anderson, R. E., 31
Apanbauer, S. J., 108
Association for Institutional Researchers Forum, 74
Astin, A. W., 37, 40

Barth, M. S., 35n
Bell Laboratories, 103
Bennett, W., 6
Bennis, W., 50
Berg, D. J., 26
Bieber, J. P., 27
Blackburn, R. T., 27
Board of directors, and cost constraints, 9–10
Boston College, 11
Boston University, 6
Bowen, H. R., 5, 8, 26, 28, 33, 36, 116
Bowen, W. G., 23
Breneman, D., 28
Brinkman, P. T., 2, 23, 25, 34, 115, 116
Bryn Mawr, 96
Byrnes, L., 112

Cage, M. C., 90
Calhoun, T. J., 35n
California, University of, at Berkeley, 10
Center for Planning Information, cost containment survey by, 13–20
Centralization, and cost-effectiveness, 53–54
Cheit, E., 90
Clark, B. R., 27, 37
Coate, L. E., 109
Cohn, E., 25

College and University Library Association, 13
College Board survey, 40
Columbia University, 12
Consolidation, for cost-effectiveness, 52–53
Contracting for services, for cost-effectiveness, 55
Cornesky, R. A., 3, 74, 83, 103, 112, 118
Cost constraints: and campus constituencies, 8–10; future of, 20–21; self-discipline as, 11–12; unavailability of money as, 10–11
Cost containment: and cost factors, 32–33; survey on, 2, 13–20; at University of Delaware, 61–74
Cost crunch, behavior in, 12
Cost disease, 29
Cost escalation, perception of, 6–8
Cost factors, 23: and cost containment, 32–33; overview of, 23–24; ratchet-and-lattice framework for, 61–62; within higher education community, 26–29; within institutions, 24–26; within society at large, 30–32
Cost reduction, administrative: at small institutions, 56–58; strategies for, 50–51
Cost-effectiveness, improving administrative, 51–56
Costs, higher education, 2, 116–117; factors influencing, 23–33; future of, 20–21; increase in, 5–6; long-term solutions for, 117–119; perception of escalation in, 6–8; of quality, 106–107; types of, 23

Daly, R. F., 28
Davies, B., 23
Davies, G. K., 1
Decentralization, and cost-effectiveness, 53–54
Delaware, University of, productivity analysis and cost containment strategy of, 61–74
Delaware County Community College, Total Quality Management at, 109–110

ORDERING INFORMATION

NEW DIRECTIONS FOR INSTITUTIONAL RESEARCH is a series of paperback books that provides planners and administrators in all types of academic institutions with guidelines in such areas as resource coordination, information analysis, program evaluation, and institutional management. Books in the series are published quarterly in spring, summer, fall, and winter and are available for purchase by subscription as well as by single copy.

SUBSCRIPTIONS for 1992 cost $45.00 for individuals (a savings of 20 percent over single-copy prices) and $60.00 for institutions, agencies, and libraries. Please do not send institutional checks for personal subscriptions. Standing orders are accepted.

SINGLE COPIES cost $14.95 when payment accompanies order. (California, New Jersey, New York, and Washington, D.C., residents please include appropriate sales tax.) Billed orders will be charged postage and handling.

DISCOUNTS for quantity orders are available. Please write to the address below for information.

ALL ORDERS must include either the name of an individual or an official purchase order number. Please submit your order as follows:
   Subscriptions: specify series and year subscription is to begin
   Single copies: include individual title code (such as IR1)

MAIL ALL ORDERS TO:
   Jossey-Bass Publishers
   350 Sansome Street
   San Francisco, California 94104

FOR SALES OUTSIDE OF THE UNITED STATES CONTACT:
   Maxwell Macmillan International Publishing Group
   866 Third Avenue
   New York, New York 10022

OTHER TITLES AVAILABLE IN THE
NEW DIRECTIONS FOR INSTITUTIONAL RESEARCH SERIES
Patrick T. Terenzini, Editor-in-Chief
Ellen Earle Chaffee, Associate Editor

U.S. Postal Service

STATEMENT OF OWNERSHIP, MANAGEMENT AND CIRCULATION
Required by 39 U.S.C. 3685

1A. Title of Publication		1B. PUBLICATION NO.							2. Date of Filing
NEW DIRECTIONS FOR INSTITUTIONAL RESEARCH		0	9	8	–	9	3	0	10/16/92

3. Frequency of Issue	3A. No. of Issues Published Annually	3B. Annual Subscription Price
Quarterly	Four (4)	$45 (individual) $60 (institutional)

4. Complete Mailing Address of Known Office of Publication (Street, City, County, State and ZIP+4 Code) (Not printers)

350 Sansome Street, San Francisco, CA 94104-1310

5. Complete Mailing Address of the Headquarters of General Business Offices of the Publisher (Not printer)

(above address)

6. Full Names and Complete Mailing Address of Publisher, Editor, and Managing Editor (This item MUST NOT be blank)

Publisher (Name and Complete Mailing Address)

Jossey-Bass Inc., Publishers (see above address at 4.)

Editor (Name and Complete Mailing Address)

Patrick T. Terenzini, Center for the Study of Higher Education, The
Pennsylvania State University, 403 South Allen St., Suite 104, University
Managing Editor (Name and Complete Mailing Address)   Park, Pennsylvania 16801-5202

Lynn Luckow, President, Jossey-Bass Inc., Publishers (see above address at 4.)

7. Owner (If owned by a corporation, its name and address must be stated and also immediately thereafter the names and addresses of stockholders owning or holding 1 percent or more of total amount of stock. If not owned by a corporation, the names and addresses of the individual owners must be given. If owned by a partnership or other unincorporated firm, its name and address, as well as that of each individual must be given. If the publication is published by a nonprofit organization, its name and address must be stated.) (Item must be completed.)

Full Name	Complete Mailing Address
Maxwell Communications Corp., plc	Headington Hill Hall
	Oxford OX30BW
	U.K.

8. Known Bondholders, Mortgagees, and Other Security Holders Owning or Holding 1 Percent or More of Total Amount of Bonds, Mortgages or Other Securities (If there are none, so state)

Full Name	Complete Mailing Address
See address at 7.	See address at 7.

9. For Completion by Nonprofit Organizations Authorized To Mail at Special Rates (DMM Section 423.12 only)
The purpose, function, and nonprofit status of this organization and the exempt status for Federal income tax purposes (Check one)

(1) ☐ Has Not Changed During Preceding 12 Months	(2) ☐ Has Changed During Preceding 12 Months	If changed, publisher must submit explanation of change with this statement.)

10.	Extent and Nature of Circulation (See instructions on reverse side)	Average No. Copies Each Issue During Preceding 12 Months	Actual No. Copies of Single Issue Published Nearest to Filing Date
A.	Total No. Copies (Net Press Run)	1900	1632
B.	Paid and/or Requested Circulation 1. Sales through dealers and carriers, street vendors and counter sales	341	104
	2. Mail Subscription (Paid and/or requested)	932	1047
C.	Total Paid and/or Requested Circulation (Sum of 10B1 and 10B2)	1273	1151
D.	Free Distribution by Mail, Carrier or Other Means Samples, Complimentary, and Other Free Copies	59	148
E.	Total Distribution (Sum of C and D)	1332	1299
F.	Copies Not Distributed 1. Office use, left over, unaccounted, spoiled after printing	568	333
	2. Return from News Agents	-0-	-0-
G.	TOTAL (Sum of E, F1 and 2—should equal net press run shown in A)	1900	1632

11. I certify that the statements made by me above are correct and complete	Signature and Title of Editor, Publisher, Business Manager, or Owner *[signature]* Larry Ishii Vice-President

PS Form 3526, Feb. 1989   (See instructions on reverse)